Hezekiah Butterworth

Zigzag Journeys in Northern Lands

The Rhine to the Arctic

Hezekiah Butterworth

Zigzag Journeys in Northern Lands
The Rhine to the Arctic

ISBN/EAN: 9783744744072

Printed in Europe, USA, Canada, Australia, Japan

Cover: Foto ©Andreas Hilbeck / pixelio.de

More available books at **www.hansebooks.com**

ZIGZAG JOURNEYS

IN

NORTHERN LANDS.

THE RHINE TO THE ARCTIC.

A SUMMER TRIP OF THE ZIGZAG CLUB THROUGH HOLLAND, GERMANY, DENMARK, NORWAY, AND SWEDEN.

BY

HEZEKIAH BUTTERWORTH,

AUTHOR OF "YOUNG FOLKS' HISTORY OF AMERICA," "YOUNG FOLKS' HISTORY OF BOSTON,"
"ZIGZAG JOURNEYS IN EUROPE," ETC.

FULLY ILLUSTRATED.

BOSTON:
ESTES AND LAURIAT,
301-305 WASHINGTON STREET.

PREFACE.

THIS fifth volume of the Zigzag books, in which history is taught by a supposed tour of interesting places, might be called a German story-book.

It was the aim of "ZIGZAG JOURNEYS IN EUROPE" and "ZIGZAG JOURNEYS IN CLASSIC LANDS" to make history interesting by stories and pictures of places. It was the purpose of "ZIGZAG JOURNEYS IN THE ORIENT" to explain the Eastern Question, and of "ZIGZAG JOURNEYS IN THE OCCIDENT" to explain Homesteading in the West.

The purpose of this volume is the same as in "EUROPE" and "CLASSIC LANDS." A light narrative of travel takes the reader to the places most conspicuously associated with German history, tradition, literature, and art, and in a disconnected way gives a view of the most interesting events of those Northern countries that once constituted a great part of the empire of Charlemagne.

It is the aim of these books to stimulate a love of history, and to *suggest* the best historical reading. To this end popular stories and pictures are freely used to adapt useful information to the tastes of the young. But in every page, story, and picture, right education and right influence are kept in view.

In this volume many German legends and fairy stories have been used, but they are so introduced and guarded as not to leave a wrong impression upon the minds of the young and immature.

H. B.

CONTENTS.

Chapter		Page
I.	The River of Story and Song	15
II.	Ghost Stories	21
III.	A Story-telling Journey	40
IV.	German Stories	60
V.	The Second Meeting of the Club	76
VI.	Night Second	92
VII.	Evening the Third	104
VIII.	Evening the Fourth	122
IX.	Fifth Meeting for Rhine Stories	145
X.	Night the Sixth	165
XI.	Cologne	184
XII.	Hamburg	206
XIII.	The Bells of the Rhine	221
XIV.	The Songs of the Rhine	253
XV.	Copenhagen	277
XVI.	Norway	288
XVII.	The Greater Rhine	309

ILLUSTRATIONS.

	PAGE		PAGE
Carrying Siegfried's Body . . *Frontispiece.*		Peasant's House in the Black Forest	95
Introducing Christianity into the North	16	Von Moltke	97
Castle in Rhine Land	17	Fountain at Schaffhausen	99
Tower of Rüdesheim on the Rhine	19	The Old Woman's Directions	101
Mountain Scenery in Southern Germany	23	The Hen and the Trench	102
"I 've seen de Debble"	26	Strasburg Cathedral	105
Cat and Rat	27	Platform of Strasburg Cathedral	107
Grandmother Golden	29	Thus didst thou to the Vase of Soissons	109
The Frightened Irishman	30	Street in Strasburg	111
Duncan Asleep	34	Clovis	113
Witches	35	Monsieur Lacombe and the Organ	115
The Grand-Ducal Castle, Schwerin	41	"Here is an Odd Treasure"	120
Ancient German Houses	43	Palace at Heidelberg	123
Ancient Religious Rites of the Peasants	45	German Student	126
Old Fortress on the Rhine	50	Castle at Heidelberg	127
St. Dunstan and the Devil	53	German Students	131
The Murder of Edward	58	Entrance to Heidelberg Castle	135
The Emperor William and Napoleon III.	63	Little Mook	137
William before his Father	64	Amputation	139
King William's Helmet	65	The Queer Old Lady who went to College	140
Jamie at the Strange-looking House	67	"And it told to her the Truth"	141
Mountain Scene in Germany	69	"Not very, very plain"	141
Jamie rushing towards his Mother	71	"They you straightway in invite"	141
The Dwarf and the Goose	72	"He of the Philosophie"	143
Eberhard	74	A Battle between Franks and Saxons	146
Bridge in the Via Mala	77	Luther's House	147
John Huss	79	A tribe of Germans on an Expedition	149
Bismarck	81	The Murder of Siegfried	151
Peter in the Forest	86	Mayence	153
Peter and the Manikin	88	Bishop Hatto and the Rats	155
Peter surpassed the King of Dancers	89	View on the Rhine	158
Peter and the Giant	90	The Lorelei	159
A Village in the Black Forest	93		

ILLUSTRATIONS.

	PAGE		PAGE
Herman's Eyes were fixed on the Rock	163	Above the Town	241
Ehrenbreitstein	166	Old Peasant Costume	244
Goethe's Promenade	167	The Old City	245
Faust Signing	171	Old Peasant Costume	247
Faust and Mephistopheles	172	Old Peasant Costumes	248
A Cleft in the Mountains	175	City Gate	249
Voltaire	179	The Neckar	250
The Unnerved Hussar	182	An Old German Town	255
Cathedral of Cologne	185	The Rhinefels	257
The Mysterious Architect	189	Mayence in the Olden Time	262
St. Martin's Church, Cologne	193	Beethoven's Home at Bonn	268
Charlemagne in the School of the Palace	197	A City of the Rhine	271
Charlemagne inflicting Baptism upon the Saxons	201	The River of Song	274
		The Palace of Rosenborg	278
The Germans on an Expedition	203	View of Copenhagen	279
Canal in Hamburg	207	Palace of Fredericksborg	283
The Palace in Berlin	209	The King in the Bag	286
Grotto	211	Gustavus Adolphus	289
Sans-Souci	213	Death of Gustavus and his Page	293
Peter the Wild Boy	217	Cascade in Norway	297
The Silent Castles	223	Lazaretto	299
Hotel de Ville, Ghent	225	The Naero Fiord	300
Bell-Tower, Ghent	228	Lake in Norway	303
Castle at Heidelberg	229	The Coast	307
Breslau	233	Niagara Falls	311
Finishing the Bell	236	A New England in the West	315
At the Inn	237	Near Quebec	317
The Day of Execution	238		

ZIGZAG JOURNEYS IN NORTHERN LANDS.

ZIGZAG JOURNEYS

IN

NORTHERN LANDS.

CHAPTER I.

THE RIVER OF STORY AND SONG.

THE Rhine! River of what histories, tragedies, comedies, legends, stories, and songs! Associated with the greatest events of the history of Germany, France, and Northern Europe; with the Rome of Cæsar and Aurelian; with the Rome of the Popes; with the Reformation; with the shadowy goblin lore and beautiful fairy tales of the twilight of Celtic civilization that have been evolved through centuries and have become the household stories of all enlightened lands!

A journey down the Rhine is like passing through wonderland; wild stories, quaint stories, legendary and historic stories, are associated with every rood of ground from the Alps to the ocean. It is a region of the stories of two thousand years. The Rhine is the river of the poet; its banks are the battle-fields of heroes; its forests and villages the fairy lands of old.

When Rome was queen of the world, Cæsar carried his eagles over the Rhine; Titus sent a part of his army which had conquered Jerusalem to the Rhine; Julian erected a fortress on the Rhine; and Valentinian began the castle-building that was to go on for a thousand years.

The period of the Goths, Huns, Celts, and Vandals came,— the conquerors of Rome; and the Rhine was strewn with Roman ruins. Charlemagne cleared away the ruins, and began anew the castle-build-

INTRODUCING CHRISTIANITY INTO THE NORTH.

ing. A Christian soldier in one of the legions that destroyed Jerusalem and tore down the temple, first brought the Gospel to the Rhine. His name was Crescaitius. He was soon followed by missionaries of the Cross. Christianity was established upon the Rhine soon after it entered Rome.

The great conquests of modern history are directly or indirectly associated with the wonderful river: Cæsar, who conquered the world, crossed the Rhine; Attila, who conquered the city of the Cæsars; Clovis, who founded the Christian religion in France; and Charlemagne, who established the Christian church in Germany. Frederick

CASTLE IN RHINE LAND.

Barbarossa and Frederick the Great added lustre to its growing history, and Napoleon gave a yet deeper coloring to its thrilling scenes.

When the Northern nations shattered the Roman power, people imagined that the dismantled castles of the Rhine became the abodes of mysterious beings: spirits of the rocks, forests, fens; strange

TOWER OF RÜDESHEIM ON THE RHINE.

maidens of the red marshes; enchanters, demons; the streams were the abodes of lovely water nymphs; the glens of the woods, of delightful fairies.

Into these regions of shadow, mystery, of heroic history, of moral conflicts and Christian triumphs, it is always interesting to go. It is especially interesting to the American traveller, for his form of Christianity and republican principles came from the Rhine. Progress to him was cradled on the Rhine, like Moses on the Nile. In the Rhine lands Luther taught, and Robinson of Leyden lived and prayed; and from those lands to-day comes the great emigration that is peopling the golden empire of America in the West. "I would be proud of the Rhine were I a German," said Longfellow. "I love rivers," said Victor Hugo; "of all rivers I prefer the Rhine."

It is our purpose in this story-telling volume to relate why the Zigzag Club was led to make the Rhine the subject of its winter evening study, and to give an account of an excursion that some of its members had made from Constance to Rotterdam and into the countries of the North Sea.

"All hail, thou broad torrent, so golden and green,
Ye castles and churches, ye hamlets serene,
Ye cornfields, that wave in the breeze as it sweeps,
Ye forests and ravines, ye towering steeps,
Ye mountains e'er clad in the sun-illumed vine!
Wherever I go is my heart on the Rhine!

"I greet thee, O life, with a yearning so strong,
In the maze of the dance, o'er the goblet and song.
All hail, beloved race, men so honest and true,
And maids who speak raptures with eyes of bright blue!
May success round your brows e'er its garlands entwine!
Wherever I go is my heart on the Rhine!

"On the Rhine is my heart, where affection holds sway!
On the Rhine is my heart, where encradled I lay,
Where around me friends bloom, where I dreamt away youth,
Where the heart of my love glows with rapture and truth!
May for me your hearts e'er the same jewels enshrine.
Wherever I go is my heart on the Rhine!"

WOLFGANG MÜLLER.

CHAPTER II.

GHOST STORIES.

THE ZIGZAG CLUB AGAIN. — SOME "GHOST" STORIES.

HE Academy had opened again. September again colored the leaves of the old elms of Yule. The Blue Hills, as lovely as when the Northmen beheld them nearly nine hundred years ago, were radiant with the autumn tinges of foliage and sky, changing from turquoise to sapphire in the intense twilight, and to purple as the shades of evening fell.

The boys were back again, all except the graduating class, some of whom were at Harvard, Brown, and Yale. Master Lewis was in his old place, and Mr. Beal was again his assistant.

The Zigzag Club was broken by the final departure of the graduating class. But Charlie Leland, William Clifton, and Herman Reed, who made a journey on the Rhine under the direction of Mr. Beal, had returned, and they had been active members of the school society known as the Club.

We should say here, to make the narrative clear to those who have not read "Zigzag Journeys in Classic Lands" and "Zigzag Journeys in the Orient," that the boys of the Academy of Yule had been accustomed each year to form a society for the study of the history, geography, legends, and household stories of some chosen country, and during the long summer vacation as many of the society as could do so, visited, under the direction of their teachers, the lands about which they had studied. This society was called the Zigzag Club, because it aimed to visit historic places without regard to direct routes of travel. It zigzagged in its travels from the associations of one historic story to another, and was influenced by the school text-book or the works of some pleasing author, rather than the guide-book.

The Zigzag books have been kindly received;[1] and we may here remark parenthetically that they do not aim so much to present narratives of travel as the histories, traditions, romances, and stories of places. They seek to tell stories at the places where the events occurred and amid the associations of the events that still remain. The Zigzag Club go seeking what is old rather than what is new, and thus change the past tense of history to the present tense.

Charlie Leland was seated one day on the piazza of the Academy, after school, reading Hawthorne's "Twice-Told Tales." Master Lewis presently took a seat beside him; and "Gentleman Jo," whom we introduced to our readers in "Zigzags in the Occident," was resting on the steps near them.

Gentleman Jo was the janitor. He was a relative of Master Lewis, and a very intelligent man. He had been somewhat disabled in military service in the West, and was thus compelled to accept a situation at Yule that was quite below his intelligence and personal worth. The boys loved and respected him, sought his advice often, and sometimes invited him to meetings of their Society.

"Have you called together the Club yet?" asked Master Lewis of Charlie, when the latter had ceased reading.

"We had an informal meeting in my room last evening."

"What is your plan of study?"

"We have none as yet," said Charlie. "We are to have a meeting next week for the election of officers, and for literary exercises we have

[1] More than one hundred thousand volumes have been sold.

agreed to relate historic *ghost stories*. We asked Tommy Toby to be present, and he promised to give us for the occasion his version of 'St. Dunstan and the Devil and the Six Boy Kings.' I hardly know what the story is about, but the title sounds interesting."

"What made you choose ghost stories?" asked Master Lewis, curiously.

"You gave us Irving and Hawthorne to read in connection with our lessons on American literature. 'Rip Van Winkle,' 'Sleepy Hollow,' and 'Twice-Told Tales' turned our thoughts to popular superstitions; and, as they made me chairman, I thought it an interesting subject just now to present to the Club."

"More interesting than profitable, I am thinking. Still, the subject might be made instructive and useful as well as amusing."

"Did you ever see a ghost?" asked Charlie of Gentleman Jo, after Master Lewis left them.

"We thought we had one in our house, when I was living with my sister in Hingham, before the war. Hingham used to be famous for its ghost stories; an old house without its ghost was thought to lack historic tone and finish."

Gentleman Jo took a story-telling attitude, and a number of the pupils gathered around him.

GENTLEMAN JO'S GHOST STORY.

I shall never forget the scene of excitement, when one morning Biddy, our domestic, entered the sitting-room, her head bobbing, her hair flying, and her cap perched upon the top of her head, and exclaimed : "Wurrah ! I have seen a ghoust, and it's lave the hoose I must. Sich a night ! I 'd niver pass anither the like of it for the gift o' the hoose. Bad luck to ye, an' the hoose is haunted for sure."

"Why, Biddy, what have you seen?" asked my sister, in alarm.

"Seen ? An' sure I did n't see nothin'. I jist shet me eyes and hid mesilf under the piller. But it was awful. An' the way it clanked its chain ! O murther !"

This last remark was rather startling. Spirits that clank their chains have a very unenviable reputation.

"Pooh!" said my uncle. "What you heard was nothing but rats." Then, turning to me, he asked: "Where is the steel trap?"

"Stolen, I think," said I. "I set it day before yesterday, and when I went to look to it it was gone."

"An' will ye be givin' me the wages?" said Biddy, "afore I bid ye good-marnin'?"

"Going?" asked my sister, in astonishment.

"An' sure I am," answered Biddy. "Ye don't think I 'd be afther stayin' in a house that 's haunted, do ye?"

In a few minutes I heard the front door bang, and, looking out, saw our late domestic, with a budget on each arm, trudging off as though her ideas were of a very lively character.

A colored woman, recently from the South, took Biddy's place that very day, and was assigned the same room in which the latter had slept.

We had invited company for that evening, and some of the guests remained to a very late hour.

The sound of voices subsided as one after another departed, and we were left quietly chatting with the few who remained. Suddenly there was a mysterious movement at one of the back parlor doors, and we saw two white eyes casting furtive glances into the room.

"What 's wanted?" demanded my sister, of the object at the door.

"I 'VE SEEN DE DEBBLE."

Our new domestic appeared in her night clothes.

"O missus, I 've seen de debble, I done have," was her first exclamation.

This, certainly, was not a sight that we should wish any one to see in our house, as desirable as a dignified spectre might have been.

"Pooh!" said my sister. "What a silly creature! Go back to bed and to sleep, and do not shame us by appearing before company in your night clothes."

"I don't keer nothing about my night clothes," she replied, with spirit. "Jes' go to de room and git de things dat belong to me, an' I 'll leave, and never disturb you nor dis house any more. It 's dreadful enough to be visited by dead folks, any way, but when de spirits comes rattling a chain it's a dreadful bad sign, you may be sure."

"What did you see?" asked I.

"See? I didn't see nothin'. 'T was bad enough to hear it. I wouldn't hav' seen it for de world. I'll go quick — jest as soon as you gets de things."

We made her a bed on a lounge below stairs. The next morning she took her bundles and made a speedy exit.

We had a maiden aunt who obtained a livelihood by visiting her relations. On the morning when our last domestic left she arrived, bag and baggage, greatly to our annoyance. We said nothing about the disturbances to her, but agreed among ourselves that she should sleep in the haunted chamber.

That night, about twelve o'clock, the household were awakened by a piercing scream above stairs. All was silent for a few minutes, when the house echoed with the startling cry of "Murder! Mur*der!* Mur*der!*" The accent was very strong on the last syllable in the last two words, as though the particular force of the exclamation was therein contained.

I hurried to the chamber and asked at the door what was the matter.

"I have seen an apparatus," exclaimed my aunt. "Mur*der!* Oh, wait a minute. I'm a dead woman."

She unlocked the door in a delirious way and descended to the sitting-room, where she sat sobbing for a long time, declaring that she was a dead woman. *She* had heard his chain rattle.

And the next morning she likewise left.

We now felt uneasy ourselves, and wondered what marvel the following night would produce. I examined the room carefully during the day, but could discover no traces of anything unusual.

That night we were again awakened by noises that proceeded from the same room. They seemed like the footfalls of a person whose feet were clad in iron. Then followed sounds like a scuffle.

I rose, and, taking a light, went to the chamber with shaky knees and a palpitating heart. I listened before the door. Presently there was a movement in the room as of some one dragging a chain. My courage began to ebb. I was half resolved to retreat at once, and on the morrow advise the family to quit the premises.

But my better judgment at last prevailed, and, opening the door with a nervous hand, I saw an "apparatus" indeed.

Our old cat, that I had left accidentally in the room, had in her claws a large rat, to whose leg was attached the missing trap, and to the trap a short chain.

"I knew the story would end in that way," said Charlie. "But that is not a true colonial ghost story, if it did happen in old Hingham."

The sun was going down beyond the Waltham Hills. The shadows of the maples were lengthening upon the lawns, and the chirp of the crickets was heard in the old walls. Charlie seemed quite dissatisfied with Gentleman Jo's story. The latter noticed it.

"My story does not please you?" said Gentleman Jo.

"No; I am in a different mood to-night."

Master Lewis smiled.

Just then a quiet old lady, who had charge of a part of the rooms in the Academy, appeared, a bunch of keys jingling by her side, much like the wife of a porter of a lodge in an English castle.

"Grandmother Golden," said Charlie, — the boys were accustomed to address the chatty, familiar old lady in this way, — "you have seen ghosts, have n't you? What is the most startling thing that ever happened in your life?"

Grandmother Golden had seated herself in one of the easy piazza chairs. After a few minutes she was induced to follow Gentleman Jo in an old-time story.

GRANDMOTHER GOLDEN'S ONLY GHOST STORY.

The custom in old times, when a person died, was for some one to sit in the room and watch with the dead body in the night, as long as it remained in the house. A good, pious custom it was, in my way of thinking, though it is not common now.

Jemmy Robbin was a poor old man. They used to call him "Auld Robin Gray," after the song, and he lived and died alone. His sister Dorothea — Dorothy she was commonly called — took charge of the house after his death, and she sent for Grandfather Golden to watch one night with the corpse.

We were just married, grandfather and I, and he wanted I should watch with him, for company; and as I could not bear that he should be out of my sight a minute when I could help it, I consented. I was young and foolish then, and very fond of grandfather, — we were in our honeymoon, you know.

We did n't go to the house at a very early hour of the evening; it was n't customary for the watchers to go until it was nearly time for the family to retire.

GRANDMOTHER GOLDEN.

In the course of the evening there came to the house a traveller, — a poor Irishman, — an old man, evidently honest, but rather simple, who asked Dorothy for a lodging.

He said he had travelled far, was hungry, weary, and footsore, and, if turned away, knew not where he could go.

It was a stormy night, and the good heart of Dorothy was touched at the story of the stranger, so she told him that he might stay.

After he had warmed himself and eaten the food she prepared for him, she asked him to retire, saying that she expected company. Instead of going with him to show where he was to sleep, as she ought to have done, she directed him to his room, furnished him with a light, and bade him good-night.

The Irishman, as I have said, was an old man and not very clear-headed. Forgetting his directions, and mistaking the room, he entered the chamber where lay the body of poor Jemmy Robbin. In closing the door the light was blown out. He found there was what seemed to be some other person in the bed, and, supposing him a live bedfellow, quietly lay down, covered himself with a counterpane, and soon fell asleep.

About ten o'clock grandfather and I entered the room. We just glanced at the bed. What seemed to be the corpse lay there, as it should. Then grandfather sat down in an easy-chair, and I, like a silly hussy, sat down in his lap.

We were having a nice time, talking about what we would do and how happy we should be when we went to housekeeping, when, all at once, I heard a snore. It came from the bed.

"What's that?" said I.

"That?" said grandfather. "Mercy! that was Jemmy Robbin."

We listened nervously, but heard nothing more, and at last concluded that it was the wind that had startled us. I gave grandfather a generous kiss, and it calmed his agitation wonderfully.

We grew cheerful, laughed at our fright, and were chatting away again as briskly as before, when there was a noise in bed. We were silent in a moment. The counterpane certainly moved. Grandfather's eyes almost started from his head. The next instant there was a violent sneeze.

I jumped as if shot. Grandfather seemed petrified. He attempted to ejaculate something, but was scared by the sound of his own voice.

"Mercy!" says I.

"What was it?" said grandfather.

"Let's go and call Dorothy," said I.

"She would be frightened out of her senses."

"I shall die with fright if I hear anything more," I said, half dead already with fear.

Just then a figure started up in the bed.

"And wha — and wha — and wha — " mumbled the object, gesticulating.

I sprang for the door, grandfather after me, and, reaching the bottom of the

stairs at one bound, gave vent to my terrors by a scream, that, for aught I know, could have been heard a mile distant.

Both of us ran for Dorothy's room. There was a sound of feet and a loud ejaculation of "Holy Peter! The man is dead!"

"It's comin'," shouted grandfather, and, sure enough, there were footsteps on the stairs.

"Dorothy! Dorothy!" I screamed.

Dorothy, startled from her sleep, came rushing to the entry in her night-dress.

"I have seen a ghost, Dorothy," said I.

"A what?"

"I have seen the awfullest —"

"It's comin'," said grandfather.

"Holy Peter!" said an object in the darkness. "There's a dead man in the bed!"

"Why, it's that Irishman," said Dorothy, as she heard the voice.

"What Irishman?" asked I. "A murdered one?"

"No; he — there — I suspect that he mistook his room and went to bed with poor Jemmy."

The mystery now became quite clear. Grandfather looked anything but pleased, and declared that he would rather have seen a ghost than to have been so foolishly frightened.

"Is that all?" asked Charlie.

"That is all," said Grandmother Golden. "Just hear the crickets chirp. Sounds dreadful mournful."

"I have been twice disappointed," said Charlie. "Perhaps, Master Lewis, you can tell us a story before we go in. Something fine and historic."

"In harmony with books you are reading?"

"And the spirit of Nature," added Charlie.

"How fine that there boy talks," said Grandmother Golden. "Get to be a minister some day, I reckon."

"How would the *True* Story of Macbeth answer?" asked Master Lewis.

"That would be excellent: Shakspeare. The greatest ghost story ever written."

"And if you don't mind, I'll just wait and hear that story, too," said good-humored Grandmother Golden.

MASTER LEWIS'S STORY OF MACBETH.

More than eight hundred years ago, when the Roman wall divided England from Scotland, when the Scots and Picts had become one people, and when the countries of Northern Europe were disquieted by the ships of the Danes, there was a king of the Scots, named Duncan. He was a very old man, and long, long after he was dead, certain writers discovered that he was a very good man. He had two sons, named Malcolm and Donaldbain.

Now, when Duncan was enfeebled by years, a great fleet of Danes, under the command of Suene, King of Denmark and Norway, landed an army on the Scottish coast. Duncan was unable to take the field against the invaders in person, and his sons were too young for such a trust. He had a kinsman, who had proved himself a brave soldier, named Macbeth. He placed this kinsman at the head of his troops; and certain writers, long, long after the event, discovered that this kinsman appointed a relation of his own, named Banquo, to assist him. Macbeth and Banquo defeated the Danes in a hard-fought battle, and then set out for a town called Forres to rest and to make merry over their victory.

A thane was the governor of a province. The father of Macbeth was the thane of Glamis.

There lived at Forres three old women, whom the people believed to be witches. When these old women heard that Macbeth was coming to the place they went out to meet him, and awaited his coming on a great heath. The first old woman saluted him on his approach with these words: "All hail, Macbeth — hail to thee, thane of Glamis!"

And the second: "All hail, Macbeth — hail to thee, thane of Cawdor!"

And the third: "All hail, Macbeth — thou shalt be king of Scotland!"

Macbeth was very much astonished at these salutations; he expected to become thane of Glamis some day, and he aspired to be king of Scotland, but he had never anticipated such a disclosure of his destiny as this. The old women told Banquo that he would become the father of kings, and then they vanished, according to Shakspeare, "into the air."

Macbeth and Banquo rode on very much elevated in spirits, when one met them who informed them that the thane of Glamis was dead. The melancholy event was not unwelcome to Macbeth; his spirits rose to a still higher pitch; one thing that the old women had foretold had speedily come to pass, — he was indeed thane of Glamis.

As Macbeth drew near the town, a glittering court party came out to welcome the army. They hailed Macbeth as thane of Cawdor. He was much surprised at this, and asked the meaning. They told him that the thane of Cawdor had rebelled, and that the king had bestowed the province upon him. Macbeth was immensely delighted at this intelligence, feeling quite sure that the rest of the prophecy would come to pass, and that he would one day wear the diadem.

Now the wife of Macbeth was a very wicked woman, and the prophecy of the witches quite turned her head, so that she could think of nothing but becoming queen. She was much concerned lest the nature of her husband should prove "too full of the milk of human kindness" to come to the "golden round." So she decided that should an opportunity offer itself for an interview with the king, she would sómewhat assist in the fulfilment of the last prophecy.

Then Macbeth made a great feast in the grand old castle of Inverness, and invited the king. Lady Macbeth thought this a golden opportunity for accomplishing the decrees of destiny, and when the old king arrived she told Macbeth that the time had come for him to strike boldly for the crown. As Shakspeare says: —

"*Macbeth.* My dearest love, Duncan comes here to-night.
Lady M. And when goes hence?
Macbeth. To-morrow.
Lady M. O never shall sun that morrow see."

When this dreadful woman had laid her plot for the taking off of Duncan, she went to the banquet-hall and greeted the royal guest with a face all radiant with smiles, and called him sweet names, and told him fine stories, and brimmed his goblet with wine, so that he thought, we doubt not, that she was the most charming creature in all the world.

It was a stormy night, thăt of the banquet; it rained, it thundered, and the wind made dreadful noises in the forests, which events, we have noticed in the stories of the old writers, were apt to occur in early times when something was about to happen. We are also informed that the owls hooted, which seems probable, as owls were quite plenty in those days.

Duncan was conducted to a chamber, which had been prepared for him in great state, when the feast was done. Before retiring he sent to "his most kind hostess" a large diamond as a present; he then fell asleep "in measureless content."

When all was still in the castle Lady Macbeth told her husband that the hour for the deed had come. He hesitated, and reminded her of the consequences if he should fail. She taunted him as being a coward, and told him to "screw his courage up to the sticking-place, and he would not fail." Then he took his dagger, and, according to Shakspeare, made a long speech over it, a speech which, I am sorry to say, stage-struck boys and girls have been mouthing in a most unearthly manner ever since the days of Queen Bess.

Macbeth "screwed his courage up to the sticking-place" indeed, and then and there was the end of the life of Duncan. When the deed was done, he put his poniard into the hand of a sentinel, who was sleeping in the king's room, under the influence of wine that Lady Macbeth had drugged.

When the meal was prepared on the following morning, Macbeth and his lady pretended to be much surprised that the old king did not get up. Macduff, the thane of Fife, who was one of the royal party, decided at last to go to the king's apartment to see if the king was well. He returned speedily in great

WITCHES.

excitement, as one may well suppose. As Shakspeare continues the interesting narrative: —

"*Macduff.* O horror! horror! horror!
Macbeth. What's the matter?
Macd. Confusion now hath made his masterpiece. Most sacrilegious murder hath broke ope the Lord's anointed temple and stole thence the life o' the building.
Macb. What is 't you say? the life?"

Macbeth appeared to be greatly shocked by the event, and, with a great show of fury and many hot words, he despatched the sentinels of the king, whom he feigned to believe had done the deed. Lady Macbeth fell upon the floor, pretending, of all things in the world for a woman of such mettle, to faint.

So Macbeth came to the throne. But he remembered that the weird women had foretold that Banquo should become the father of kings, which made him fear for the stability of his throne. He thought to correct the tables of destiny somewhat, and so he induced two desperate men to do by Banquo as he had done by Duncan. The spirit of Banquo was not quiet like Duncan's, but haunted him, and twice appeared to him at a great feast that he gave to the thanes.

Now Banquo had a son named Fleance, whom the murderers were instructed to kill, but who, on the death of his father, eluded his enemies and fled to France. The story-writers say that the line of Stuart was descended from this son.

Macbeth, like all wicked people who accomplish their ends, was very unhappy. He lived in continual fear lest some of his relations should do by him as he had done by Duncan and Banquo. He became so miserable at last that he decided to consult the witches who had foretold his elevation, to hear what they would say of the rest of his life.

He found them in a dark cave, in the middle of which was a caldron boiling. The old women had put into the pot a toad, the toe of a frog, the wool of a bat, an adder's tongue, an owl's wing, and many other things, of which you will find the list in Shakspeare. Now and then they walked around the pot, repeating a very sensible ditty: —

"Double, double, toil and trouble;
Fire, burn; and, caldron, bubble."

They at last called up an apparition, who said that Macbeth should never be overcome by his enemies until Birnam wood should come to the castle of Dunsinane, the royal residence, to attack it.

"Macbeth shall never vanquished be until
Great Birnam wood to high Dunsinane hill
Shall come against him."

Now, Birnam wood was twelve miles from Dunsinane (pronounced Dunsnan), and Macbeth thought that the language was a mystical way of saying that he always would be exempt from danger.

Malcolm, the son of Duncan, the rightful heir to the throne, was a man of spirit, and he went to England to solicit aid of the good King Edward the Confessor against Macbeth. Macduff, having quarrelled with the king, joined Malcolm, and the English king, thinking favorably of their cause, sent a great army into Scotland to discrown Macbeth.

When this army reached Birnam wood, on its way to Dunsinane, Macduff ordered the men each to take the bough of a tree, and to hold it before him as he marched to the attack, that Macbeth might not be able to discover the number and the strength of the assailants. Thus Birnam wood came against Dunsinane. When Macbeth saw the sight his courage failed him, and he saw that his hour had come. A battle ensued, in which he was conquered and killed.

Such is the story, and it seems a pity to spoil so good a story; but I fear that Shakspeare made his wonderful plot of much the same "stuff that dreams are made of."

Duncan was a grandson of Malcolm II. on his father's side, and Macbeth was a grandson of the same king, though on the side of his mother. On the death of Malcolm, in 1033, each claimed the throne. Macbeth, according to rule of Scottish succession, had the best claim, but Duncan obtained the power. Macbeth was naturally dissatisfied, and the insolence of Malcolm, the son of Duncan, who placed himself at the head of an intriguing party in Northumberland, changed his dissatisfaction to resentment, and he slew the king. He once had a dream, which he deemed remarkable, in which three old women met him and hailed him as thane of Cromarty, thane of Moray, and finally as king. Upon this light basis genius has built one of the most powerful tales of superstition in the language.

Duncan was slain near Elgin, and not in the castle of Inverness. Malcolm avenged his father's death, slaying Macbeth at a place called Lumphanan, and not at Dunsinane, as recorded in the play.

And then Sir Walter Scott finds that "Banquo and his son Fleance" never had any real existence, which leaves no material out of which to construct a ghost.

"So there were no witches, after all?" said Charlie.

"No; no witches."

"No Banquo?"
"No Banquo."
"No ghost?"
"No ghost. Banquo never lived."
"Is that all?" asked Grandmother Golden.
"That is all."

CHAPTER III.

A STORY-TELLING JOURNEY.

THE CLUB REORGANIZED. — THE RHINE AND THE LANDS OF THE BALTIC. — TOMMY
TOBY'S STORY OF THE SIX BOY KINGS.

T the first formal meeting of the Club Charlie Leland was chosen President. He was the intellectual leader among the boys, now that the old Class had gone; he was a lad of good principles, bright, generous, and popular. As may be judged from the somewhat discursive dialogue on the piazza, he had a subject well matured in his mind for the literary exercises of the Club.

"We all like stories," he said, "and the Rhine lands are regions of stories, as are the countries of the Baltic Sea. The tales and traditions of the Rhine would give us a large knowledge of German history, and, in fact, of the great empire of Europe, over which Charlemagne ruled, and which now is divided into the kingdoms of Northern Europe. The stories of haunted castles, spectres, water nymphs, sylvan deities, and fairies, if shapes of fancy, are full of instruction, and I know of no subject so likely to prove intensely interesting as the Rhine and the Baltic; and I would like to propose it to the Club for consideration, although, owing to my position as President, I do not make a formal motion that it be adopted."

Charlie's picturesque allusion to the myths of the Rhine and the Baltic seemed to act like magic on the minds of the Club; and a formal

THE GRAND-DUCAL CASTLE, SCHWERIN.

ANCIENT GERMAN HOUSES.

motion that the Rhine and the Baltic be the subject of future literary meetings was at once made, seconded, and unanimously adopted.

Master Lewis had entered the room quietly while the business of the Club was being thus happily and unanimously carried forward. The boys had asked him to be present at the meeting, and to give them his opinions of their plans.

"I think," he said, "that your choice of a subject for your literary evenings is an excellent one, but I notice a tendency to place more stress on the fine old fictions of Germany and the North than upon actual history. These fictions for the most part grew out of the disturbed consciences of bad men in ignorant and barbarous times. They were shapes of the imagination."

He continued : —

"Let me prepare your minds a little for a proper estimate of these alluring and entertaining stories."

MASTER LEWIS ON POPULAR SUPERSTITIONS.

The front of Northumberland House, England, used to be ornamented with the bronze statue of a lion, called Percy. A humorist, wishing to produce a sensation, placed himself in front of the building, one day, and, assuming an attitude of astonishment, exclaimed : —

"It wags, it wags!"

His eyes were riveted on the statue, to which the bystanders readily observed that the exclamation referred. Quite a number of persons collected, each one gazing on the bronze figure, expecting to see the phenomenon. Their imagination supplied the desired marvel, and presently a street full of people fancied that they could see the lion Percy wag his tail!

An old distich runs something as follows : —

"Who believe that there are witches, there the witches are ;
Who believe there are n't no witches, are n't no witches there."

There is much more good sense than poetry in these lines. The marvels of superstition are witnessed chiefly by those who believe in them.

The sights held as supernatural are usually not more wonderful than those that arise from a disordered imagination. The spectres of demonology are not more fearful than those shapes of fancy produced by opium and dissipation ; and

ANCIENT RELIGIOUS RITES OF THE PEASANTS.

the visions of the necromancer are not more wonderful than those that arise from a fever, or even from a troubled sleep.

Yet it is a fact, and a very singular one, that, however at random the fancies of unhealthy intellects may appear on ordinary subjects, those fancies obtain a greater or less credit when they touch upon supernatural things. Instances of monomaniacs (persons insane on a single subject) who have imagined things quite as marvellous as the most superstitious, but whose illusions have been treated with the greatest ridicule, might be cited almost without limit.

I once knew of an elderly lady, who thought that she was a goose. Making a nest in one corner of the room, she put in it a few kitchen utensils, which she supposed to be eggs, and began to incubate. She found the process of incubation, in her case, a very slow one; and her friends, fearing for her health, called in a doctor. He endeavored to reason with her, but she only replied to his philosophy by stretching out her neck, which she seemed to think was a remarkably long one, and hissing. The old lady had a set of gilt-band china cups and saucers, which, in her eyes, had been a sort of household gods. The knowledge of the fact coming to the ears of the physician, he advised her friends to break the precious treasures, one after another, before her eyes. The plan worked admirably. She immediately left her nest, and ran to the rescue of the china, and the excitement brought her back to her sense of the proprieties of womanhood.

Another old lady, who also resided in a neighboring town, fancied she had become a veritable teapot. She used to silence those who attempted to reason with her by the luminous argument, " See, here (crooking one arm at her side) is the handle, and there (thrusting upward her other arm) is the spout!" What could be more convincing than that?

Another lady, whose faculties had begun to decline, thought her toes were made of glass; and a comical figure she cut when she went abroad, picking up and putting down her feet with the greatest caution, lest she should injure her precious toes.

Now these cases provoke a smile; but, had these ancient damsels fancied that they were bewitched, or that they were haunted, or that they held communion with the spirits of the invisible world, instead of exciting laughter and pity, they would have occasioned no small excitement among the simple-minded people of the neighborhood in which each resided.

A young Scottish farmer, having been to a fair, was riding homeward on horseback one evening over a lonely road.

He had been drinking rather freely at the fair, according to the custom, and his head was far from steady, and his conscience far from easy.

It was moonlight, and he began to reflect what a dreadful thing it would be to meet a ghost. His fears caused him to look very carefully about him. As he was approaching the old church in Teviotdale, he saw a figure in white standing on the wall of the churchyard, by the highway.

The sight gave him a start, but he continued his journey, hoping that it was his imagination that had invested some natural object with a ghostly shape. But the nearer he approached, the more ghostlike and mysterious did the figure appear.

He stopped, hesitating what to do, and then concluded to ride slowly. There was no other way to his home than the one he was following. He knew well enough that his mind was somewhat unsettled by drinking, and what he saw might, after all, he thought, be nothing but an illusion. He would approach the object slowly and cautiously, and, when very near it, would put spurs to his horse and dash by.

As he drew near, however, the figure showed unmistakable signs of life, gesticulating mysteriously, and uttering gibberish, that, although odd, sounded surprisingly human.

It was a ghostly night: the dim moonlight filled the silent air, and the landscape was flecked with shadows; it was a ghostly place, — Teviotdale churchyard; and, in perfect keeping with the time and place, stood the figure, doing as a ghost is supposed to do, — talking gibberish to the moon.

The young man's nerves were quite unstrung as he put spurs to his horse for a rush by the object of his fright. As he dashed past, his hair almost bristling with apprehension, the supposed phantom leaped upon the back of the horse and clasped the frightened man about his waist. His apprehensions were startling enough before, but now he was wrought to the highest pitch of terror.

He drove his spurs into his horse, and the animal flew over the earth like a phantom steed. Such riding never before was seen in the winding road of Teviotdale.

In a wonderfully short time the reeking animal stood trembling and panting before his master's gate. The young man called lustily for his servants, who, coming out, were commanded in frantic tones to "Tak aff the ghaist, tak aff the ghaist!" And "tak aff the ghaist" they did, which proved to be a young lady well known in Teviotdale for her unfortunate history.

She had married an estimable young man, to whom she was very strongly attached, and the brightest worldly prospects seemed opening before her. Her husband was taken ill, and suddenly died. She had confided in him so fondly that the world lost its attractions for her on his decease, and she moodily dwelt upon her misfortune until she became deranged.

Her husband was buried in Teviotdale churchyard, and she was in the habit of stealing away from her friends at night, to weep over his grave. These melancholy visits had the effect of giving a new impetus to her malady, making her for a time the victim of any fancy that chanced to enter her mind.

On the night of our story she imagined that the young farmer was her husband, and awaited his approach with great exhilaration of spirits, determined to give him an affectionate greeting.

The fright came near costing the young man his life. He was taken from his saddle to his bed, where he lay for weeks prostrated by a high nervous fever.

An eminent writer, after relating the above authentic story, remarks: —

"If this woman had dropped from the horse unobserved by the rider, it would have been very hard to convince the honest farmer that he had not actually performed a part of his journey with a ghost behind him."

True. Teviotdale churchyard would have obtained the reputation of being haunted, and would have been a terror to weak-minded people for many years to come.

The ignorant and simple are not alone subject to illusions of fancy. The great and learned Pascal, than whom France has produced no more worthy philosopher, believed that an awful chasm yawned by his side, into which he was in danger of being thrown. This dreadful vision, with other fancies as gloomy, cast a shadow over an eventful period of his life, and gave a dark coloring to certain of his writings. Yet Pascal, on most subjects, was uncommonly sound in judgment. How unfavorable might have been the influence, had his disorder assumed a different form, and placed before him the delusion of a ghost!

Before giving credit to stories of supernatural events, even from sources that seem to be trustworthy, I hope my young friends will consider duly how liable to error are an unhealthy mind and an excited imagination. Every man is not a knave or a cheat who claims to have witnessed unnatural phenomena, but the judgment of very excellent persons is liable to be infected by illusions of the imagination.

I do not say that we may not receive impressions from the spiritual world. As the geologist, the botanist, the chemist, sees things in nature that the unschooled and undeveloped do not see, so it may be that a spiritually educated mind may know more of the spiritual world than the gross and selfish mind. I will not enlarge upon this topic or discuss this question; it might not be proper for me so to do.

Master Lewis had aimed to make clear to the boys that it is easy to start a superstitious story, and to suggest that such stories in ignorant times became *legends*.

OLD FORTRESS ON THE RHINE.

"I propose," said Willie Clifton, "that the first seven meetings of the Club be devoted to the Rhine."

"We might call this series of meetings *Seven Nights on the Rhine*," added Herman Reed.

"The old members of the Club who made the Rhine journey with Mr. Beal might give us an account of that journey," suggested one of the new boys.

The plans suggested by these remarks met with approval, and a committee was appointed to arrange the literary exercises for seven meetings of the Club, to be known as *Seven Nights on the Rhine*.

The literary exercises for the present evening consisted of the relation of historic ghost stories, chiefly by members of the old Club. Among these were the Province House Stories of Hawthorne, the tradition of Mozart's Requiem, the Cock Lane Ghost, and several incidents from Scott's novels.

The principal story, however, was given by Tommy Toby, an old member of the Club, and a graduate of the Academy.

TOMMY TOBY'S STORY OF ST. DUNSTAN AND THE DEVIL AND THE SIX BOY KINGS.

A splendid court had Athelstane, and foreign princes came there to be educated. Among these princes was Louis, the son of Charles the Simple, of France, who, by his long residence in England, obtained the pretty name of *Louis d'Outremer*.

Splendid weddings were celebrated there. The king married one of his sisters to the King of France, another to the Emperor of Germany, another to Hugo the Great, Count of Paris, and another to the Duke of Aquitaine.

After the fight with the Cornish men, all of the land was at peace for many years, and the nobility became very scholarly and the people very polite.

Athelstane had a favorite, a friar, who made more mischief in his day and generation than any other man. This man is known in history by the name of St. Dunstan.

When Dunstan was a boy, he was taken very ill of a fever. One night, being delirious, he got up from his bed, and walked to Glastonbury church, which was then repairing, and ascended the scaffolds and went all over the building ; and because he did not tumble off and break his neck, people said that he had performed the feat under the influence of inspiration, being directed by an angel.

This was called Dunstan's first miracle.

When he recovered from the fever, and heard of the miracle that he was said to have wrought, he was greatly pleased, and thought to turn the good opinion of people to his own advantage by performing other miracles.

So he made a harp that played in the wind, — now soft, now loud ; now sweet, now solemn. He said that the harp played itself. The people heard the sounds, full of seeming expression, as though touched by airy fingers, and, as they could not discredit the evidence of their own ears, they too reported that the harp played itself. And great was the fame of Dunstan's harp.

But Dunstan, according to old history, became a very bad man; so bad that I cannot tell you the worst things that he did. He discovered his true character at last, notwithstanding his sweetly playing harp.

He pretended to be a magician. Now a magician, in those old times, was one who was supposed to know things beyond the reach of common minds, who pretended to calculate the influence of the stars on a person's destiny, and who understood the effects of poisonous vegetables and minerals. The Saxon magicians were chiefly nobles and monks, and all of their great secrets which are worth knowing are now understood as simple matters of science, even by schoolboys.

Athelstane's conscience must have been rather restless, I fancy, concerning young Edwin, his brother, whom he caused to be drowned ; and people with unquiet conscience are usually very superstitious. At any rate, he made a bosom friend of Dunstan, after the latter took up the black art, and became greatly interested in magic, much to the sorrow of the people.

At last a party of the king's friends resolved that the bad influence of the wily prelate should come to an end. They waylaid him one dark night, in an unfrequented place, and, binding him hand and foot, threw him into a miry marsh. But the water was shallow, and Dunstan kept his nose above the mire, and, after shouting lustily for help, and floundering about for a long time, he succeeded in getting out, to make a great deal of noise and trouble in the world, and we have some strange stories to tell you about him yet.

Athelstane died in the year 940, and he was succeeded upon the throne by his half-brother, Edmund, who was the first of the six boy kings.

Edmund was eighteen years of age when he took his place on the honorable Saxon throne of Alfred the Great. He was a high-spirited young man, warm-hearted and brave. He conquered Cumberland from the Ancient Britons, and protected his kingdom against the fierce sea-kings of the North. Like his great ancestor, King Alfred, he was fond of learning and art. He improved and adorned public places and buildings. He made a very elegant appearance, and held a showy court, and they called him the Magnificent.

But Edmund was fond of convivial suppers, and used himself to drink deeply of wine. He lived fast, and his friends lived fast, though they appeared to live very happily and merrily.

But young men given to festive suppers and to wine are not apt to make a long history; and the history of Edmund the Magnificent, the first boy king, was a short one.

Edmund was succeeded in the year 946 by Edred, his brother, a well-meaning youth, who was the second of the six boy kings of England.

Dunstan had become abbot of Glastonbury Abbey, the church where he performed the miracle when he was sick of the fever. He was very ambitious to meddle in affairs of state, but his bad name had weakened his influence with Edmund, and it seemed likely to do the same with well-intentioned Edred. He desired to create a public impression again that he was a saint.

He retired to a cell and there spent his time working very hard as a smith, and — so the report went — in devotion.

Then the people said: "How humble and penitent Dunstan is! He has the back-ache all day, and the leg-ache all night, and he suffers all for the cause of purity and truth."

ST. DUNSTAN AND THE DEVIL.

Then Dunstan told the people that the Devil came to tempt him, which, with his aches for the good cause, made his situation very trying.

The Devil, he said, wanted him to lead a life of selfish gratification, but he would not be tempted to do a thing like that; he never thought of himself, — oh, no, good soul, not he.

The people said that Dunstan must have become a very holy man, or the Devil would not appear to him bodily.

One day a great noise was heard issuing from the retreat of this man, and filling all the air for miles, the like of which was never known before. The people were much astonished. Some of them went to Dunstan to inquire the cause. He told them a story of a miracle more marvellous than any that he had previously done.

The Devil came to him, he said, as he was at work at his forge, and tempted him to lead a life of pleasure. He quickly drew his pincers from the fire, and seized his tormentor by the nose, which put him in such pain that he bellowed so lustily as to shake the hills. The people said that it was the bellowing of the Evil One that they had heard.

This wonderful story ended to Dunstan's liking, for the artful do flourish briefly sometimes.

The boy king Edred was in ill-health, and suffered from a lingering illness for years. He felt the need of the counsel of a good man. He said to himself, —

"There is Dunstan, a man who has given up all selfish feelings and aspirations, a man whom even the Devil cannot corrupt. I will bring him to court, and will make him my adviser."

Then pure-hearted Edred brought the foxy prelate to his court, and made him — of all things in the world! — the royal treasurer.

Edred died in the year 955, having for nine years aimed to do justly and to govern well. His decease, like his brother's before him, was sincerely lamented.

He left a well-ordered government, except in the department of the treasury. Some remarkable "irregularities" — as stealing is sometimes called nowadays — had taken place there, some of the public money having become mixed up with Dunstan's.

The next of the six boy kings of England was Edwy the Fair, — fifteen years of age when he ascended the throne.

He was the son of Edmund, — a handsome boy, and as good at heart as he was handsome. Though so young, he had married a beautiful princess, named Elgiva. So we have here a boy king and a girl queen.

As if one bad prelate were not enough, there was, besides Dunstan, another great mischief-maker, Odo, the Dane, Archbishop of Canterbury.

The coronation of Edwy was the occasion of great rejoicing. They had a sumptuous feast in the evening, attended by all the prelates and thanes. Edwy liked the society of the girl queen better than that of these rude people, and in the midst of the festivities he retired to the queen's apartment to see her and the queen mother.

Odo, the archbishop, noticed that the boy king had left his place at the tables. He rightly guessed the reason, and deemed such conduct disrespectful to himself and to the guests. So he went and made complaint to Dunstan, and Dunstan went to look for the missing king. When the latter came to the queen's apartment, and was refused admittance, he broke open the door, upbraided Edwy for his absence from the feast, and, seizing him by the collar, dragged and pushed him roughly back to the banqueting-hall.

Edwy, of course, resented this treatment. Dunstan replied by accusing him of great impropriety, and talked in a very overbearing way, and Edwy, though a considerate boy, and of a mild disposition, at last lost his temper.

"You have a very nice sense of propriety," he said. "You were the treasurer in the last reign, I believe. I intend to call you to account for the way that you fulfilled your trust."

Dunstan was greatly astonished, and, guilty man that he was, he began to feel very unsafe.

The boy king made the attempt which he had threatened, to call Dunstan to account for his late doings in the treasury. But the latter, when he found that Edwy was in earnest, fled to Ghent.

The nobles saw somewhat into his true character when he thus disappeared from court, and a party of men was sent in pursuit of him to put out his eyes. But he was too foxy to be caught, and arrived safely in Belgium at last, to make a great deal of trouble in the world yet.

Incited by Dunstan, Odo raised a rebellion. When he had drawn to himself a sufficient party to insure his personal safety, he proclaimed Edgar, the younger brother of Edwy, king.

Dunstan returned to England, and joined Odo, and this precious pair soon discovered the value of their piety, as you shall presently see.

Edwy the Fair loved the girl queen. She was beautiful as well as amiable, and was as devoted to her husband as she was lovely. Odo and Dunstan wished to break the spirit of Edwy, and thought to accomplish their end by capturing the queen. They caused her to be stolen from one of the royal palaces, and her cheeks to be burned with hot irons, in order to destroy the beauty that had so enchanted the boy king. They then sent her to Ireland, and sold her as a slave.

The Irish people pitied the weeping maiden, and loved her. They healed the scars on her cheeks, that the hot irons had made. When her beauty returned, she grew light-hearted again, and all her dreams were of the king.

Then the Irish people released her from bondage, and gave her money to return to Edwy.

She entered England full of joyful anticipations, and made rapid journeys towards the place where Edwy held his court. But Odo and Dunstan, who had been apprised of her coming, intercepted her, and ordered that she should be tortured and put to death. They caused the cords of her limbs to be severed, so that she was unable to walk or move. The beautiful girl survived the cutting and maiming but a few days.

Weeping continually over her disappointments and sorrows, and shrieking at times from the acuteness of her pain, she died at Gloucester, — perhaps the most unfortunate princess who ever came to the English throne.

When Edwy heard of her death, he ceased to struggle for his right; he cared for nothing more. He grew paler and thinner day by day, his beauty faded, his thoughts turned heavenward, and he aspired to a better crown and kingdom. He died of a broken heart before he reached the age of twenty, having aimed for three years to govern well.

Edwy's short reign was followed by that of his brother Edgar, who succeeded to the Anglo-Saxon throne in the year 959, and was an unprincipled and dissolute king.

He was fifteen years of age when he began to reign. One of his first acts was to reward the intriguing Dunstan for his crimes by bestowing upon him the archbishopric of Canterbury. Think of conferring an archbishopric as the price of a brother's ruin and death! Ah, better to be Edwy the Fair in his early grave, with the birds singing and the violets waving above him, than the cruel boy Edgar upon the throne.

He resigned the government almost wholly to Dunstan, his primate, and spent his time in gayety, pleasure, and ease. He was unstable, profligate, and vicious. He once broke into a convent and carried off a beautiful nun, named Editha. For this violation of the sanctuary, Dunstan commanded him not to wear his crown for seven years, which was no great punishment, as he could ornament his head as well in some other way.

Dunstan certainly possessed great ability as a statesman. He employed the vast armaments of England against the neighboring sovereigns, and compelled the King of Scotland and the Princes of Wales, of the Isle of Man, and of the Orkneys, to do homage to Edgar.

The boy king annually made a voyage around England in great state, accompanied by princes and nobles.

On one of these occasions, when he wished to visit the Abbey of St. John the Baptist, on the River Dee, he appointed eight crowned kings to pull the oars of his barge, while he himself acted as steersman.

The vainglorious young sovereign then went into the grand old abbey and said his prayers, after which he returned in the same pomp, rowed by the eight subject kings.

This event is celebrated in the songs and ballads of the olden time, which tell of the glory of England, when the eight crowns glimmered on the sun-covered waters of the Dee.

Edgar, who was King of England up to the year 975, married twice, and left two sons. The elder of these was named Edward, the son of a good queen, Ethelfreda; the other was named Ethelred, the son of the bad queen, Elfrida.

Edward had the best claim to the throne, but the intriguing Elfrida endeavored to secure the succession to her own son, Ethelred, a boy about seven years old. Dunstan decided against her, and caused Edward to be crowned. The boy king was at this time thirteen years of age.

He was an amiable, susceptible boy, loving every one, and wishing every one well, and believing, with childish simplicity, that all the world was as pure at heart and as unselfish as himself.

But Elfrida hated him, and resolved that his reign should be a short one, if it was within the reach of her arts to make it so.

She retired with little Ethelred to Crofe Castle, a beautiful country seat in Dorsetshire. Green forests waved around it, and blue hills seemed to semicircle the sky. The silver horn of the hunter often echoed through the stream-cleft woodlands, and merrily blew before the castle gate.

Edward and a youthful court party went hunting one day in the dreamy old forests of Dorsetshire. Chancing to ride near Crofe Castle, Edward thought that he would like to see Elfrida and his little brother. So he separated himself from his attendants, rode to the castle, and blew his horn.

Elfrida presently appeared, her face glowing with smiles.

"Thou art welcome, dear king," she said, in a winning way. "Pray dismount and come in, and we will have pleasant talk and good cheer."

"No, madam," said Edward. "My company would notice my absence, and think that some evil had befallen me. Please bring me a cup of wine, and I will drink to your health and to my little brother's, in my saddle, and then I must away with speed."

Elfrida turned away to order the wine. She gave another order at the same time in a whisper to an armed attendant.

The wine was brought. Elfrida filled the cup and handed it to the boy king. As he held it up it sparkled in the light. Elfrida stood in the gateway, holding little Ethelred by the hand.

"Health," said Edward, putting the bright cup to his lips.

There crept up behind him softly an armed man, whose muscles stood out like brass, and whose eyes burned like fire. He sprang upon the boy king and stabbed him in the back. The affrighted horse dashed away, dragging the bleeding body by the stirrup, — on, on, on, over rut and rock, bush and brier.

They tracked him by his blood. They found his broken body at last. They took it up tenderly and with many tears, and laid it beneath the moss and fern.

THE MURDER OF EDWARD.

When little Ethelred saw his brother stabbed and bleeding, and dragged over the rough earth, he began to weep. Elfrida beat him and sent him to his chamber.

What a night was that when the moon silvered the forest! One boy king mangled and dead on the cold ground, and another boy king weeping in the forest castle, and beaten and bruised for being touched at heart at the murder of his bright, innocent brother.

Ethelred came to the English throne at the age of ten. He was the last of the six boy kings.

The people held him in disfavor from the first on account of his bad mother, and when Dunstan put the crown on his head at Kingston, he pronounced a curse instead of a blessing. Neither the blessing nor the curse of a man like

Dunstan could be of much account, and we do not believe that the latter did the little boy Ethelred any harm.

Dunstan was now old and as full of craft and wickedness as he was full of years. He continued to practise jugglery, which he called performing miracles, whenever he found his influence declining, or had an important end to accomplish.

In the reign of Ethelred Dunstan died. As he had used politics to help the church, he was made a saint. This was in a rude and ignorant age.

Poor boy kings! Edmund was murdered; Edwy died of a broken heart; Edward was stabbed and dragged to death at his horse's heels; and Ethelred lost his kingdom. Three of them were good and three were bad. Only one of them was happy.

Edmund, eighteen years of age, reigned from 940 to 946; Edred, 946 to 955; Edwy, fifteen years of age, 955 to 958; Edgar, fifteen years of age, 958 to 975; Edward, thirteen years of age, 975 to 979; Ethelred, ten years of age, 979 to 1016.

So the boy kings reigned in all seventy-six years, and governed England in their youth for nearly fifty years.

"I like your story, Master Toby," said Master Lewis; "as a story, I mean. The historic facts are mainly as you have given them, but I think St. Dunstan's intentions may have been good, after all. He lived in an age of superstition, when it was believed that any political act was right that would increase the power of the church. Christianity then was not what it had been in the early church nor what it is to-day. Men must be somewhat regarded in the light of the times in which they lived."

The literary exercises for the evening were thus closed.

CHAPTER IV.

GERMAN STORIES.

The Story of the Emperor William. — The Story of "Sneeze with Delight." — Poem-Stories.

T the first meeting of the Club to study the history and to relate stories of the Rhine and the North, Master Lewis was present, and, after the preliminary business had been transacted, said that he had some suggestions in mind which he wished to make.

"I notice," he said, "that many of you have been obtaining from the Boston Public Library English translations of the works of Hauff, Hoffman, Baron de La Motte Fouqué, Grimm, Schiller, and Tieck, and I think that there is danger that story-reading and story-telling may occupy too much of your time and thought. Let me propose that a brief history of each author be given with the story at the meetings of the Club, so that you may at least obtain some knowledge of German literature."

The suggestion met with the approval of all, and it was voted that at future meetings the biographies of authors should be given with the stories, and that only the stories of the best authors should be selected, except in the case of legends of places.

"I have another proposal to make," said Master Lewis. "You are not very familiar with German politics. Suppose you let me give you from time to time some short talks about the German Government and its ministers, — King William, Count Bismarck, and Count Von Moltke."

This kind offer was received with cheers and placed upon record with thanks.

"Perhaps you may be willing to open our exercises to-night with one of the talks you have planned," said the President. "It would be a helpful beginning, which we would appreciate."

"I am not as well prepared as I would like," said the teacher; "but as I believe in making a first meeting of this kind a sort of a model in its plan and purpose, I will in a free way tell you something of

THE STORY OF THE EMPEROR WILLIAM.

The life of the Emperor of Germany has been full of thrilling and dramatic scenes.

When he was a boy, Germany — the great Germany of Charlemagne — was divided into states, each having its own ruler. His father was Frederick William III., King of Prussia, and his mother was Louise, an excellent woman ; his youth was passed amid the excitements of Napoleon's conquests. Russia and Prussia combined against Napoleon ; Russia was placed at a disadvantage in two doubtful battles, when she deserted the Prussian cause, and made a treaty of peace.

Napoleon then sent for the King of Prussia, to tell him what he would leave him.

The lovely Queen Louise went with the unfortunate king to meet the French conqueror, hoping thereby to obtain more favorable terms. But Napoleon treated her with scorn, boasting that he was like "waxed cloth to rain."

He, however, offered the queen a rose, in a softer moment.

"Yes," said Louise, thinking of her kingdom, "but with Magdeburg."

"It is *I* who give, and *you* who take," answered Napoleon haughtily.

Napoleon took away from Prussia all the lands on the Elbe and the Rhine, and, uniting these to other German states, formed a kingdom for his brother Jerome.

The good Queen Louise pined away with grief and shame at her country's losses, and died two years after of a broken heart. So the boyhood of William was very sad.

It is said that children fulfil the ideals of their mothers. Poor Louise little thought that her second son would one day be crowned Emperor of all Germany in the palace of the French kings at Versailles.

William was born in 1797; he ascended the throne as King of Prussia in 1861. How widely these dates stand apart!

On the day of his coronation as King of Prussia, he exhibited his own character and religious faith by putting the crown on his own head. "I rule," he said, "by the favor of God and no one else."

Under his vigorous rule Prussia grew in military power, and excited the jealousy of the French people. Napoleon III., on a slight pretext, declared war with Prussia. In this war Prussia was victorious.

A MEMORABLE HOUR.

That was indeed a memorable hour in the emperor's life when he met the fallen Emperor of the French in the Chateau Bellevue, on a hill of the Meuse overlooking Sedan. The king and the emperor had met before; they then were equals, brother rulers of two of the most powerful nations on earth. They met now as conqueror and captive, and the one held the fate of the other in his hands.

"We were both moved at seeing each other again under such circumstances," said King William. "I had seen Napoleon only three years before, at the summit of his power. What my feelings were is more than I can describe."

The king spoke first.

"God has given victory to me in the war that has been declared against me."

"The war," said Napoleon, "was not sought by me. I did not desire it. I declared it in obedience to the public sentiment of France."

"Your Majesty," said the king, "made the war to meet public opinion; but your ministers created that public opinion."

"Your artillery, sire, won the battle. The Prussian artillery is the finest in the world."

"Has your Majesty any conditions to propose?"

"None: I have no power; I am a prisoner."

"Where is the government in France with which I can treat?"

"In Paris: the empress and the ministers. I am powerless."

King William, as you know, marched to Paris, and at last made conditions of peace almost as hard as Napoleon I. had made with his father. The German princes in his hour of victory offered him the crown of Southern Germany, and he was crowned at Versailles, in the great hall of mirrors, Emperor of Germany.

Let me now speak of the kaiser's

MILITARY CAREER.

It is rare that men and women live to celebrate their seventy-fifth birthday. The age allotted to mortals by the Psalmist is threescore and ten. But the hale old Emperor of Germany has not only recently commemorated

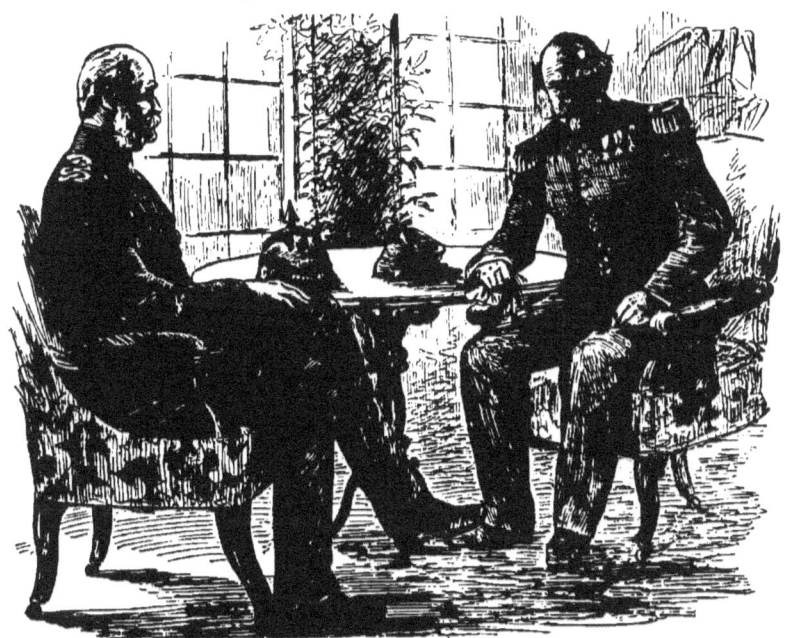

THE EMPEROR WILLIAM AND NAPOLEON III.

the completion of his eighty-sixth year, but — what is still more striking — at the same time marked the seventy-sixth year of his service as an officer in the Prussian army.

It is related that, on the 22d of March, 1807, on which day William was just ten years old, his father, then King of Prussia, called him into his study and said, —

"My son, I appoint you an officer in my army. You will serve in Company No. 1 of the First Guard Regiment."

The little prince drew himself up, gave his father a prompt military salute, and retired. An hour later he reappeared before the king, attired in the uniform of his new rank; and, repeating the salute, announced to his royal father that "he was ready for duty."

Even at so early an age, William was no fancy soldier, holding rank and title, and leaving to

WILLIAM BEFORE HIS FATHER.

humbler officers the duties and hardships. He at once devoted himself to the task of a junior ensign; and from that time onward became an officer in truth, laboring zealously to master the military science, and rising step by step, not by favor, but by merit and seniority.

At the age of eighteen, William was in Blucher's army at Waterloo, taking an active part in the overthrow of Napoleon, and witnessing that mighty downfall. A little later, he was promoted to the rank of major for cool courage under heavy fire; and from that time on, for nearly half a century, William devoted himself wholly to the military profession.

When he ascended the Prussian throne, there was no more unpopular man in the kingdom. He had put down the revolutionary rising in Berlin with grim and relentless hand; and the people believed that their new monarch was a cruel and haughty tyrant.

It was not until after the great triumph over Austria, in 1866, that the Prussians began to discover that King William was not only a valiant soldier, but an ardent lover of his country, and a kind-hearted, whole-souled father of his people.

THE STATESMAN.

For the last sixteen years, no sovereign in Europe has been more devotedly beloved and revered by his subjects. Although William is autocratic, and believes in his "divine right" to rule as sturdily as did his mediæval ancestors, and has not a little contempt for popular clamors and popular rights, his reign has been on the whole brilliantly wise and successful. While this has been in a great measure due to the presence of a group of great men around him, — notably of Bismarck and Von Moltke, — the emperor himself has had no small share in promoting the power and towering fortunes of Germany.

His paternal ways with his people, his military knowledge, his fine, frank, hearty, chivalrous nature, his sound sense in the choice of his advisers, and his perception of the wisdom of their counsels, have much aided in raising Prussia and Germany to their present height in Europe.

KING WILLIAM'S HELMET.

Beneath his commanding and rugged exterior there beats a very kindly heart. Many incidents have been related to show the simple good-nature of his character. In his study, on the table at which he writes, there has long remained a rusty old cavalry helmet, the relic of some military association of the emperor.

Whenever the death-warrant of a condemned criminal is brought to him to sign, the emperor looks at it, and then slyly slips the fatal document under the helmet. Sometimes his ministers, anxious that the warrants should be signed, take occasion, in his absence from the study, to pull the papers out from beneath the helmet, just enough to catch their master's eye.

Most often, however William, on perceiving them, quietly pushes them back again, without a word. So great is his repugnance to dooming even a hardened criminal to death, by a mere scratch of his pen.

At eighty-six, the stalwart old kaiser cannot hope to dwell much longer among his people; but it will be very long before his fine qualities, soldierly courage, and affectionate nature will grow dim in the memory of the fatherland.

The stories related at this meeting were largely from Grimm and Fouqué, and are to be found in American books.

The most pleasing of the stories, told by Herman Reed, is not so well known, and we give it here.

SNEEZE WITH DELIGHT.

Many, many years ago there lived in an old German town a good cobbler and his wife. They had one child, Jamie, a handsome boy of some eight years. They were poor people; and the good wife, to help her husband, had a stall in the great market, where she sold fruit and herbs.

One day the cobbler's wife was at the market as usual, and her little boy was with her, when a strange old woman entered the stalls.

The woman hardly seemed human. She had red eyes, a wizened, pinched-up face, and her nose was sharp and hooked, and almost reached to her chin. Her dress was made up of rags and tatters. Never before had theré entered the market such a repulsive-looking person.

"Are you Hannah the herb-woman?" she asked, bobbing her head to and fro. "Eh?"

"Yes."

"Let me see, let me see; you may have some herbs I want."

She thrust her skinny hands into the herbs, took them up and smelled of them, crushing them as she did so.

Having mauled them to her heart's content, she shook her head, saying, —

"Bad stuff; rubbish; nothing I want; rubbish, rubbish, — eh?"

"You are an impudent old hag," said the cobbler's boy, Jamie; "you have crushed our herbs, held them under your ugly nose, and now condemn them."

"Aha, my son, you do not like my nose, — eh? You shall have one, too, to pay for this, — eh?"

"If you want to buy anything, pray do so at once," said the cobbler's wife; "you are keeping other customers away."

"I *will* buy something," said the hag viciously; "I *will* buy. I will take these six cabbages. Six? That is more than I can carry, as I have to lean upon my stick. You must let your boy take them home for me."

This was but a reasonable request, and the cobbler's wife consented.

Jamie did as he was bid, and followed the hag to her home. It was a long distance there. At last the beldam stopped in an out-of-the-way part of the town, before a strange-looking house. She touched a rusty key to the door, which flew open, and, as the two entered, a most astonishing sight was revealed to Jamie's eyes.

The interior of the house was like a throne-room in a palace, the ceilings were of marble and gold, and the furniture was jewelled ebony.

The old woman took a silver whistle and blew it. Little animals — guinea pigs and squirrels — answered the call. They were dressed like children, and walked on two legs; they could talk and understand what was said to them. Was the beldam an enchantress, and were these little animals children, whom she had stolen and made victims of her enchantments?

"Sit down, child," said the old woman, in a soft voice, "sit down; you have had a heavy load to carry. Sit down, and I will make you a delicious soup; one that you will remember as long as you live. It will contain some of the herb for which I was looking in the market and did not find. Sit down."

The beldam hurried hither and thither, and with the help of the guinea pigs and squirrels quickly made the soup.

"There, my child, eat that. It contains the magic herb I could not find in the market. Why did your mother not have it? Whoever eats that will become a magic cook."

Jamie had never tasted such delicious soup. It seemed to intoxicate him. It produced a stupor. He felt a great change coming over him. He seemed to become one of the family of guinea pigs and squirrels, and, like them, to serve their mistress. Delightful little people they were, — he came to regard them as brothers ; and time flew by.

Years flew by, and other years, when one day the dame took her crutch and went out. She left her herb-room open, and he went in. In one of the secret cupboards he discovered an herb that had the same scent as the soup he had eaten years before. He examined it. The leaves were blue and the blossoms crimson. He smelt of it.

He began to sneeze, — such a delightful sneeze! He smelt, and sneezed again. Suddenly he seemed to awake, as from a dream, — as though some strange enchantment had been broken.

"I must go home," he said. "How mother will laugh when I tell her my dream! I ought not to have gone to sleep in a strange house."

He went out into the street. The children and idlers began to follow him.

"Oho, oho! look, what a strange dwarf! Look at his nose! Never the like was seen before."

Jamie tried to discover the dwarf, but could not see him.

He reached the market. His mother was there, a sad old woman, in the same place. She seemed altered ; looked many years older than when he left her. She leaned her head wearily on her hand.

"What is the matter, mother dear?" he asked.

She started up.

"What do you want of me, you poor dwarf? Do not mock me. I have had sorrow, and cannot endure jokes."

"But, mother, what has happened?"

He rushed towards her to embrace her, but she leaped into the air.

The market-women came to her and drove him away.

He went to his father's cobbler's shop. His father was there, but he looked like an old man.

"Good gracious! what is that?" said he wildly, as Jamie appeared.

"How are you getting on, master?" asked Jamie.

"Poorly enough. I'm getting old, and have no one to help me."

"Have you no son?"

"I *had* one, years ago."

MOUNTAIN SCENE IN GERMANY.

"Where is he now?"

"Heaven only knows. He was kidnapped one market-day, seven years ago."

"Seven years ago!"

Jamie turned away. The people on the street stared at him, and the ill-bred children followed him. He chanced to pass a barber's shop, where was a looking-glass in the window. He stopped and saw himself.

The sight filled him with terror. He was a dwarf, *with a nose like that of the strange old woman*.

What should he do?

He remembered that the old woman had said that the eating of the magic soup that contained the magic herb would make him a magic cook.

He went to the palace of the duke and inquired for the major domo. He was kindly received, as dwarfs are in such places, and he asked to be employed in the kitchen, and allowed to show his skill in preparing some of the rare dishes for the table.

No one in the ducal palace was able to produce such food as he. He was made chief cook in a little time, and enjoyed the duke's favor for two years. He grew fat, was honored at the great feasts, and became the wonder of the town.

Now happened the strangest thing of his strange life.

(Ye that have eyes, prepare to open them now.)

One morning he went to the goose market to buy some nice fat geese, such as he knew the duke would relish. He purchased a cage of three geese, but he noticed that one of the geese did not quack and gabble like the others.

"The poor thing must be sick," he said; "I will make haste to kill her."

To his great astonishment, the goose made answer: —

"Stop my breath,
And I will cause your early death."

Then he knew that the goose was some enchanted being, and he resolved to spare her life.

"You have not always had feathers on you, as now?" said the dwarf.

"No; I am Mimi, daughter of Waterbrook the Great."

"Prithee be calm; I will be your friend; I know how to pity you. I was once a squirrel myself."

Now the duke made a great feast, and invited the prince. The prince was highly pleased with the ducal dishes, and praised the cook.

"But there is one dish that you have not provided," said the prince.

"What is that?" asked the duke.

"*Pâté Suzcrain.*"

The duke ordered the dwarf to make the rare dish for the next banquet. The dwarf obeyed.

When the prince had tasted, he pushed it aside, and said, —

"There is one thing lacking, — one peculiar herb. It is not like that which is provided for my own table."

The duke, in a towering passion, sent for the dwarf.

"If you do not prepare this dish rightly for the next banquet," he said, "you shall lose your head."

Now the dwarf was in great distress, and he went to consult with the goose.

"I know what is wanting," said the goose; "it is an herb called Sneeze with Delight. I will help you find it."

The dwarf took the goose under his arm, and asked of the guard, who had

been placed over him until he should prepare the dish, permission to go into the garden.

They were allowed to go. They searched in vain for a long time; but at last the goose spied the magic leaf across the lake, and swam across, and returned with it in her bill.

"'T is the magic herb the old woman used in the soup," said the dwarf. "Thank the Fates! we may now be delivered from our enchantment."

He took a long, deep sniff of the herb. He then sneezed with delight, and lo! he began to grow, and his nose began to shrink, and he was transformed to the handsomest young man in all the land.

He took the goose under his arm, and walked out of the palace yard. He carried her to a great magician, who delivered her from her enchantment, and she sneezed three sneezes, and became the handsomest lady in all the kingdom.

Now, Mimi's father was very rich, and he loaded Jamie with presents, which were worth a great fortune.

Then handsome Jamie married the lovely Mimi; and he brought his old father and mother to live with them in a palace, and they were all exceedingly happy.

"What is the moral of such a tale as that?" asked one of the Club.

"If you have any crookedness, to find the magic herb," said Charlie.

Charlie Leland, the President, closed the exercises with some translations of his own, which he called "Stories in Verse." We give two of them here; each relates an incident of Eberhard, the good count, whom German poets have often remembered in song.

THE RICHEST PRINCE.

In a stately hall in the city of Worms,
    A festive table was laid ;
The lamps a softened radiance shed,
    And sweet the music played.

Then the Saxon prince, and Bavaria's lord,
    And the Palsgrave of the Rhine,
And Würtemberg's monarch, Eberhard,
    Came into that hall to dine.

Said the Saxon prince, with pride elate,
    "My lords, I have wealth untold :
There are gems in my mountain gorges great;
    In my valleys are mines of gold."

"Thou hast boasted well," said Bavaria's lord,
    "But mine is a nobler land :
I have famous cities, and castled towns,
    And convents old and grand."

"And better still is my own fair land,"
    Said the Palsgrave of the Rhine :
"There are sunny vineyards upon the hills ;
    In the valleys are presses of wine."

Then bearded Eberhard gently said,
"My lords, I have neither gold,
Nor famous cities, nor castled towns,
Nor convents grand and old.

"I have no vineyards upon the hills,
In the valleys no presses of wine;
But God has given a treasure to me
As noble as any of thine.

EBERHARD.

"I wind my horn on the rocky steep,
In the heart of the greenwood free,
And I safely lay me down and sleep
On any subject's knee."

Oh, then the princes were touched at heart,
And they said, in that stately hall,
"Thou art richer than we, Count Eberhard;
Thy treasure is greater than all."

EQUALITY.

The banners waved, the bugles rung,
   The fight was hot and hard;
Beneath the walls of Doffingen,
Fast fell the ranks of Suabian men
   Led on by Eberhard.

Count Ulric was a valiant youth,
   The son of Eberhard;
The banners waved, the bugles rung,
His spearmen on the foe he flung,
   And pressed them sore and hard.

"Ulric is slain!" the nobles cried, —
   The bugles ceased to blow;
But soon the monarch's order ran:
"My son is as another man,
   Press boldly on the foe!"

And fiercer now the fight began,
   And harder fell each blow;
But still the monarch's order ran:
"My son is as another man,
   Press, press upon the foe!"

Oh, many fell at Doffingen
   Before the day was done;
But victory blessed the Suabian men,
And happy bugles played again,
   At setting of the sun.

CHAPTER V.

THE SECOND MEETING OF THE CLUB.

CONSTANCE.—THE STORY OF HUSS.—BISMARCK AND THE GERMAN GOVERNMENT.— THE STORY OF THE HEART OF STONE.—POEM.—SEVEN NIGHTS ON THE RHINE: NIGHT FIRST.

HE second meeting of the Club was opened by Mr. Beal with an account of Constance, and of the great Council that convened there in 1414.

"*Via Mala!* So the old Romans called the road near the source of the Rhine. It passed over and through dark and awful chasms, that the river, as it came down from the Alps, had been tunnelling for thousands of years.

"The Rhine is the gift of the Alps, as Egypt is the gift of the Nile. From its source amid the peaks of the clouds to its first great reservoir, the Lake of Constance, it passes through one of the wildest and most picturesque regions in the world. It is not strange that the Romans should have called their old Swiss road *Via Mala*.

"Lake Constance! How our heads bent and our feelings kindled and glowed when we beheld it! It is the most beautiful lake that Germany possesses. It is walled by snow-capped mountains, whose tops seem like islands in the blue lakes of the skies. Quaint towns are nestled among the groves of the shore; towers, with bells ringing soft and melodious in the still air. The water is like emerald. Afar, zigzagging sails flap mechanically in the almost pulseless air.

"There is color everywhere, of all hues: high, rich tones of color;

low tones. Piles of gems on the mountains, gloomy shadows in the groves; a deep cerulean sky above, that the sunlight fills like a golden sea. At sunset the lake seems indeed like the vision that John saw,—'a sea of glass, mingled with fire.'

"The town of Constance, once a great city, is as old as the period of Constantine. When Charlemagne went to Rome to receive the imperial crown, he rested here. Here a long line of German kings left the associations of great festivities; here those kings passed their Christmases and Easters. Here convened brilliant regal assemblies

BRIDGE IN THE VIA MALA.

Here the ambassadors from Milan appeared before Barbarossa, and delivered to him the golden key of the Italian states.

"But these events are of comparatively small importance in comparison with the so-called Holy Council of Constance, in 1414. It was a time of spiritual dearth in the world. Arrogance governed the Church, and immorality flourished in it. There were three popes, each at war with the others, — John XXIII., Benedict XII., and Gregory XII.

"The Council was called to choose a pope, and to reform the Church. The town for four years became the centre of European history. Hither came kings and princes; the court of the world was here.

"The town filled, and filled. It was like a great fair. Delegates came from the North and the South, the East and the West. There were splendid fêtes; luxury and vainglory. At one time there were present a hundred thousand men.

"The Council accomplished nothing by way of reform, except to induce the three rival popes to relinquish their claims to a fourth; but it stained its outward glory with a crime that will never be forgotten.

"When we were in Florence, — beautiful Florence! — the tragedy of Savonarola rose before us like a spectre in the history of the past. Savonarola tried to reform the conduct of the clergy and to maintain the purity of the Church, but failed. He made the republic of Florence a model Christian commonwealth. Debauchery was suppressed, gambling was prohibited, the licentious factions of the times were there publicly destroyed. He arraigned Rome for her sins. The Roman party turned against him and accused him of heresy, the punishment of which was death. He declared his innocence, and desired to test it with his accusers by walking through a field of living fire. He believed God would protect him from the flames, like the worthies of old. His enemies were unwilling to go with him into the fiery ordeal. He was condemned and executed. The martyr of Florence in after years became one of its saints.

"At Constance a like tragedy haunted us. Constance has been called 'the city of Huss.'

"Among the mighty ones who wended their way to the city of the lake, to attend the great Council, was a pale, thin man, in mean attire. He had been invited to the Council by the Emperor Sigismund, who promised to protect his person and his life. He was a Bohemian reformer; a follower of Wycliffe. He was graciously received, but was soon after thrown into prison on the charge of heresy.

"They led him in chains before the Council, which assembled in an old hall, which is still shown. The emperor sat upon the throne as president.

"He confessed to having read and disseminated the writings of Wycliffe.

JOHN HUSS.

"He was required to denounce the English reformer as one of the souls of the lost.

"'If he be lost, then I could wish my soul were with his,' he said firmly.

"This was pronounced to be heresy.

"The emperor declared that he was not obliged to keep his word to heretics, and that his promise to protect the life of the Bohemian was no longer binding.

"He was condemned to death. He was stripped of his priestly robes, and the cup of the sacrament was taken from his hands with a curse.

"'I trust I shall drink of it this day in the kingdom of heaven,' he said.

"'We devote thy soul to the devils in hell,' was the answer of the prelates.

"He was led away, guarded by eight hundred horsemen, to a meadow without the gates. Here he was burned alive, and triumphed in soul amid the flames.

"Such was the end of John Huss, the Savonarola of Constance.

"We made an excursion upon the lake. The appearance of the old city from the water is one of the most beautiful that can meet the eye. It seems more like an artist's dream than a reality, — floating towers in a crystal atmosphere.

"'Girt round with rugged mountains,
The fair Lake Constance lies.'

"The lake is walled with mountains, and wears a chain of castle-like towns, like a necklace.

"It would be delightful to spend a summer there. Excursions on the steamers can be made at almost any time of the day. One can visit in this way five different old countries, — Baden, Würtemberg, Bavaria, Austria, and Switzerland."

Mr. Beal's succinct account of the old city led to a discussion of the gains of civilization from martyrdoms for principle and progress. He was followed by Master Lewis, who gave the Class some account of

BISMARCK AND THE GERMAN GOVERNMENT.

In the eyes of the multitude, Bismarck is a great but unscrupulous statesman, intent upon uniting Germany and making it the leading nation of Europe.

As a man, he seems hard-headed, self-willed, and iron-handed. As a ruler, he is looked upon as the incarnation of the despotic spirit,— a believer in force, an infidel as to moral suasion.

Many persons who sympathize with his policy censure the means by which he executes it. They do not consider that so long as that policy is threatened from within and without, the Chancellor must trust in force; nor do they read the lesson of the centuries,— *Force* must rule until *Right* reigns.

The fact is not apprehended by the unthinking multitude, that the work of grafting a statesman's policy into the life of a nation requires, like grafting a fruit-tree, excision, incision, pressure, and time.

But it is not of Bismarck's policy I would first speak, but of that which few credit him with possessing,— his moral convictions. Strange as it may seem to those who know only the Chancellor, Bismarck is not only a religious man, but his religion is the foundation of his policy.

Dr. Busch, one of the statesman's secretaries, in a recent book, "Bismarck in the Franco-German War," narrates incidents and reports private conversations which justify this assertion.

On the eve of his leaving Berlin to join the army, the Chancellor partook of the Lord's Supper. The solemn rite was celebrated in his own room, that it might not appear as an exhibition of official piety.

BISMARCK.

One morning Bismarck was called suddenly from his bed to see a French general. Dr. Busch, on entering the bedroom just after the chief had left it, found everything in disorder. On the floor was a book of devotion, "Daily Watchwords and Texts of the Moravian Brethren for 1870." On the table by the bed was another, "Daily Refreshment for Believing Christians."

"The Chancellor reads in them every night," said Bismarck's valet to Dr. Busch, seeing his surprise.

One day, while dining with his staff, several of whom were "free-thinkers," Bismarck turned the conversation into a serious vein. A secretary had spoken of the feeling of duty which pervaded the German army, from the private to the general.

Bismarck caught the idea and tossed it still higher. "The feeling of duty," he said, "in a man who submits to be shot dead on his post, alone, in the dark, is due to what is left of belief in our people. He knows that there is Some One who sees him when the lieutenant does not see him."

"Do you believe, Your Excellency," asked a secretary, "that they really reflect on this?"

"Reflect? no; it is a feeling, a tone, an instinct. If they reflect they lose it. Then they talk themselves out of it.

"How," Bismarck continued, "without faith in a revealed religion, in a God who wills what is good, in a Supreme Judge, and in a future life, men can live together harmoniously, each doing his duty and letting every one else do his, I do not understand."

There was a pause in the conversation, and the Chancellor then gave expression to his faith.

"If I were no longer a Christian," he said, "I would not remain for an hour at my post. If I could not count upon my God, assuredly I should not do so on earthly masters.

"Why should I," he continued, "disturb myself and work unceasingly in this world, exposing myself to all sorts of vexations, if I had not the feeling that I must do my duty for God's sake? If I did not believe in a Divine order, which has destined this German nation for something good and great, I would at once give up the business of a diplomatist. Orders and titles have no charm for me."

There was another pause, for the staff were silent before this revelation of their chief's inner life. He continued to lay bare the foundations of his statesmanship.

"I owe the firmness which I have shown for ten years against all possible absurdities only to my decided faith. Take from me this faith, and you take from me my fatherland. If I were not a believing Christian, if I had not the supernatural basis of religion, you would not have had such a Chancellor.

"I delight in country life, in the woods, and in nature," he said, in the course of the conversation. "Take from me my relation to God, and I am the man who will pack up to-morrow and be off to Varzin [his farm] to grow my oats."

The surprise with which these revelations of a statesman's inner life are read is due to their singularity. Neither history nor biography is so full of instances of statesmen confessing their faith in God and in Christianity, at a dinner-table surrounded by "free-thinkers," as to prevent the reading of these revelations from being both interesting and stimulating.

"I live among heathen," said the Chancellor, as he concluded this acknowledgment that his religion was the basis of his statesmanship. "I don't seek to make proselytes, but I am obliged to confess my faith."

Prince von Bismarck was born in 1813. His political history is similar to Emperor William's, which I related at our last meeting. The Emperor and his Chancellor, in matters of state, have been as one man. Each has aimed to secure the unity of the German empire. Each has sought to disarm, on the one hand, that branch of the Catholic party who give their allegiance to Rome rather than the government, the so-called Ultramontanes; and the Socialists, on the other hand, who would overthrow the monarchy. The two strong men have ruled with a firm hand, but with much wisdom. Germany could hardly have a more liberal government, unless she became a republic.

The stories of the evening were chiefly selected from Hoffman They were too long and terrible to be given here. Among them were "The Painter" and "The Elementary Spirit." In introducing these stories, Mr. Beal related some touching and strange incidents of their author.

HOFFMAN.

Hoffman died in Berlin. His career as a musical artist had been associated with the Prussian-Polish provinces, where he seems to have acquired habits of dissipation in brilliant but gay musical society.

Hoffman had exquisite refinement of taste, and sensitiveness to the beautiful in nature and art, but the exhilaration of the wine-cup was to him a fatal knowledge. It made him in the end a poor, despised, inferior man.

As he lost his self-mastery, he also seemed to lose his self-respect. He mingled with the depraved, and carried the consciousness of his inferiority into all his associations with better society.

"I once saw Hoffman," says one, "in one of his night carouses. He was sitting in his glory at the head of the table, not stupidly drunk, but warmed with wine, which made him madly eloquent. There, in full tide of witty discourse, or, if silent, his hawk eye flashing beneath his matted hair, sat this unfortunate genius until the day began to dawn; then he found his way homeward.

"At such hours he used to write his wild, fantastic tales. To his excited fancy everything around him had a spectral look. The shadows of fevered thought stalked like ghosts through his soul."

This stimulated life came to a speedy conclusion. He was struck with a most strange paralysis at the age of forty-six.

His disease first paralyzed his hands and feet, then his arms and legs, then his whole body, except his brain and vital organs.

In this condition it was remarked in his presence that death was not the worst of evils. He stared wildly and exclaimed, —

"Life, life, only life, — on any condition whatsoever!"

His whole hope was centred in the gay world which had already become to him as a picture of the past.

But the hour came at last when he knew he must die. He asked his wife to fold his useless hands on his breast, and, looking at her pitifully, he said, "And we must think of God also."

Religion, in his gay years, as a provincial musician, and as a poet in the thoughtless society of the capital, had seldom occupied his thoughts.

His last thought was given to the subject which should have claimed the earliest and best efforts of his life.

"God also!" It was his farewell to the world. The demons had done their work. Life's opportunities were ended.

The words of his afterthought echo after him, and, like his own weird stories, have their lesson.

Herman Reed presented a story from a more careful writer. It is a story with an aim, and left an impressive lesson on the minds of all. If it be somewhat of an allegory, it is one whose meaning it is not hard to comprehend.

THE HEART OF STONE.

The Black Forest, from time out of mind, has abounded with stories of phantoms, demons, genii, and fairies. The dark hue of the hills, the shadowy and mysterious recesses, the lonely ways, the beautiful glens, all tend to suggest the legends that are associated with every mountain, valley, and town. The old legends have filled volumes. One of the most popular of recent stories of the Black Forest is the "Marble Heart; or, the Stone-cold Heart," by Hauff.

Wilhelm Hauff, a writer of wonderful precocity, genius, and invention, was born at Stuttgart in 1809. He was designed for the theological profession, and entered the University of Tübingen in 1820. He had a taste for popular legends, and published many allegorical works. He died before he had completed his twenty-sixth year.

There once lived a widow in the Black Forest, whose name was Frau Barbara Munk. She had a boy, sixteen years old, named Peter, who was put to the trade of charcoal-burner, a common occupation in the Black Forest.

Now a charcoal-burner has much time for reflection; and as Peter sat at his stack, with the dark trees around him, he began to cherish a longing to become rich and powerful.

"A black, lonely charcoal-burner," he said to himself, "leads a wretched life. How much more respected are the glass-blowers, the clock-makers, and the musicians!"

The raftsmen of the forest, too, excited his envy. They passed like giants through the towns, with their silver buckles, consequential looks, and clay pipes, often a yard long. There were three of these timber-dealers that he particularly admired. One of them, called "Fat Hesekiel," seemed like a mint of gold, so freely did he use his money at the gaming-tables at the tavern. The second, called "Stout Schlurker," was both rich and dictatorial; and the third was a famous dancer.

These traders were from Holland. Peter Munk, the young coal-burner, used to think of them and their good fortune, when sitting alone in the pine forests. The Black Foresters were people rich in generous character and right principle, but very poor in purse. Peter began to look upon them and their homely occupations with contempt.

"This will do no longer," said Peter, one day. "I must thrive or die. Oh, that I were as much regarded as rich Hesekiel or powerful Schlurker, or even as the King of the Dancers! I wonder where they obtain their money!"

There were two Forest spirits, of whom Peter had heard, that were said to help those who sought them to riches and honor. One was Glassmanikin, a good little dwarf; and the other was Michael the Dutchman, — dark, dangerous, terrible, and powerful, — a giant ghost.

Peter had heard that there was a magic verse, which, were he to repeat it alone in the forest, would cause the benevolent dwarf, Glassmanikin, to appear. Three of the lines were well known, —

"O treasure-guarder, 'mid the forests green,
Many, full many a century hast thou seen:
Thine are the lands where rise the dusky
    pine —"

He did not know the last line, and, as he was but a poor poet, he was unable to make a line to fill the sense, metre, and rhyme.

He inquired of the Black Foresters about the missing line, but they only knew as much as he, else many of them would have called the fairy banker to their own service.

One day, as he was alone in the forest, he resolved to repeat, over and over, the magic lines, hoping that the fourth line would in some way occur to him.

"O treasure-guarder, 'mid the forests green,
Many, full many a century hast thou seen:
Thine are the regions of the dusky pine."

As he said these words he saw, to his astonishment, a little fellow peep around the trunk of a tree; but, as the fourth line did not come to him, Mr. Glassmanikin disappeared.

Peter went home, with his mind full of visions. Oh, that he were a poet! He consulted the oldest wood-cutters, but none of them could supply the missing line.

Soon after, Peter again went into the deep forest, his brain aching for a rhyme with *pine*. As he was hurrying along, a gigantic man, with a pole as big as a mast over his shoulder, appeared from behind the pine-trees. Peter was filled with terror, for he felt that it was none other than the giant-gnome, Michael the Dutchman.

"Peter Munk, what doest thou here?" he thundered.

"I want to pass this road on business," said Peter, in increasing alarm.
"Thou liest. Peter, you are a miserable wight, but I pity you. You want money. Accept my *conditions*, and I will help you. How many hundred thalers do you want?"
"Thanks, sir; but I'll have no dealings with you: I am afraid of your *conditions*. I have heard of you already."

Peter began to run.

The giant strode after him; but there was a magic circle in the forest that he could not pass, and, as he was near it, Peter was able to escape.

A great secret had been revealed to Peter, and he now thought he had the clew to the charm. The good dwarf, Glassmanikin, only helped people who were born on Sunday.

Possessed of this fact, Peter again ventured on into the deep forest. He found himself at last under a huge pine. He stopped there to rest, when suddenly a perfect line and rhyme occurred to him. He leaped into the air with joy, and exclaimed:—

> "O treasure-guarder, 'mid the forests green,
> Many, full many a century hast thou seen:
> Thine are the regions of the dusky pine,
> And children born on Sabbath-days are thine."

A little old manikin arose from the earth at the foot of the pine. He wore a black jerkin, red stockings, and a peaked hat. His face had a kindly expression, and he sat down and began to smoke a blue glass pipe.

"Peter, Peter," said the fairy, "I should be sorry to think that the love of idleness has brought you hither to me."

"No; I know that with idleness vice begins. But I would like a better trade. It is a low thing to be a charcoal-burner. I would like to become a glass-blower."

"To every Sunday-child who seeks my aid, I grant three wishes. If, however, the last wish is a foolish one, I cannot grant it. Peter, Peter, what are your wishes? Let them be good and useful."

"I wish to dance better than the King of Dancers."

"One."

"Secondly, I would always have as much money in my pocket as 'Fat Hesekiel.'"

"Oh, you poor lad!" said the gnome sadly. "What despicable things to wish for! To dance well, and have money to gamble! What is your third wish?"

"I should like to own the finest glass factory in the forest."
"O stupid Charcoal Peter! you should have wished for wisdom. Wealth is useless without wisdom to use it. Here are two thousand guldens. Go."

Peter returned home. At the frolics at the inn, he surpassed the King of Dancers in dancing, and he was hailed with great admiration by the young. He began to gamble at the ale-houses, and was able to produce as much money as Fat Hesekiel himself. People wondered. He next ordered a glass factory to be built, and in a few months Peter Munk was rich and famous and envied. People said he had found a hidden treasure.

But Peter did not know how to use his money. He spent it at the alehouse; and at last, when the money in the pockets of Fat Hesekiel, for some reason, was low, he was unable to pay his debts, and the bailiffs came to take him to prison.

In his troubles he resolved to go again into the deep forest, and seek the aid of the forest gnomes.

PETER AND THE MANIKIN.

THE SECOND MEETING OF THE CLUB. 89

"If the good little gnome will not help me," he said, "the big one will."

As he passed along, ashamed of his conduct in not having better deserved of the good fairy, he began to cry,—

"Michael the Dutchman! Michael the Dutchman!"

In a few moments the giant raftsman stood before him.

"You 've come to me at last," he said. "Go with me to my house, and I will show you how I can be of service to you."

Peter followed the giant to some steep rocks, and down into an abyss; there was the gnome's palace.

"Your difficulties come from *here*," said the gnome, placing his hands over the young man's heart. "Let me have your heart, and you shall have riches."

"Give you my heart?" said Peter; "I should die."

"No; follow me."

He led Peter into a great closet, where were jars filled with liquid. In them were the hearts of many who had become rich. Among them were the hearts of the King of the Dancers and of Fat Hesekiel.

"The hinderance to wealth is feeling. I have taken, as you see, the hearts of these rich men. I have replaced them by hearts of stone. You see how *they* flourish. *You* may do the same."

PETER SURPASSED THE KING OF DANCERS.

"A heart of stone must feel very cold within," said Peter.

"But what is the use of a heart of feeling, with poverty? Give me your heart, and I will make you rich."

"Agreed," said Peter.

The giant gave him a drug, which caused stupor. When Peter awoke from the stupor his heart seemed cold. He put his hand on his breast: there was no motion. Then he knew that he had indeed a heart of stone.

PETER AND THE GIANT.

Nothing now brought him pleasure or delight. He loved nothing; pitied no one's misfortunes. Beauty was nothing. He cared not for relatives or friends; but he had money, money.. The supply never failed.

He travelled over the world, but everything seemed dead to him. Sentiment was dead within him. He lied, he cheated. He filled many homes with wretchedness and ruin.

At last he became weary of life.

"I would give all my riches," he said, "to feel once again love in my heart."

He resolved to go into the woods and consult the good fairy.

He came to the old pine-tree, —

"O treasure-guarder, 'mid the forests green,
Many, full many a century thou hast seen;
Thine are the regions of the dusky pine,
And children born on Sabbath-days are thine."

The Glassmanikin came up again, as before. He met Peter with an injured look.

"What wouldst thou?"
"That thou shouldst give me a feeling heart."
"I cannot. I am not Michael the Dutchman."
"I can live no longer with this stone heart."
"I pity you. Take this cross, and go to Michael. Get him to give you back your heart, under some pretext, and when he demands it again show him this cross, and he will be powerless to harm you."

Peter took the cross and hurried into the deep forest. He called, —
"Michael the Dutchman! Michael the Dutchman!"

The giant appeared.

"What now, Peter Munk?"

"There is feeling in my heart. Give me another. You have been deceiving me."

"Come to my closet, and we will see."

The gnome took out the stone heart, and replaced it for a moment by the old heart from the jar. It began to beat. Peter felt joy again. How happy he was! A heart, even with poverty, seemed the greatest of blessings. He would not exchange his heart again for the world.

"Let me have it now," said the gnome.

But Peter held out the cross. The gnome shrank away, faded, and disappeared.

Peter put his hand on his breast. His heart was beating. He became a wise, thrifty, and prosperous man.

CHAPTER VI.

NIGHT SECOND.

SEVEN NIGHTS ON THE RHINE: — BASLE. — MARSHAL VON MOLTKE. — THE STORY OF THE ENCHANTED HEN.

UR second night on the Rhine was passed at Basle. Leaving Lake Constance, the Rhine, full of vivid life, starts on its way to the sea. At the Rhinefall at Schaffhausen the water scenery becomes noble and exciting. A gigantic rock, over three hundred feet wide, impedes the course of the river, and over it the waters leap and eddy and foam, and then flow calmly on amid green woods, and near villages whose windows glitter in the sun.

We rode through the so-called Forest towns. High beeches stood on each side of the river, and the waters here were as blue as the sky, and so clear we could see the gravelly bed.

The river hastened to Basle. We hastened on like the river. Basle is the first town of importance on the Rhine.

Here we obtained a fine view of the Black Forest range of hills, and beheld the distant summits of the Jura and the Vosges.

Basle was a Roman fortified town in the days of the struggles of Rome with the Barbarians. It is gray with history, — with the battles of Church and State, battles of words, and battles of deeds and blood. But the sunlight was poured upon it, and the Rhine flowed quietly by, and the palaces of peace and prosperity rose on every hand.

A VILLAGE IN THE BLACK FOREST.

as though the passions of men had never been excited there, or the soil reddened with blood.

We took a principal street on our arrival, and followed the uncertain way. It led to the cathedral, on high ground. At the en-

PEASANT'S HOUSE IN THE BLACK FOREST.

trance to the grand old church stood the figures of St. George and St. Martin on prancing horses. The interior was high and lofty, with an imposing organ. Here we read on one of the tombs, "Erasmus of Rotterdam."

The famous Black Forest is comprised within the lines of an isosceles triangle, which has Basle and Constance at each end of the line of base. The Rhine turns toward the north at Basle, and very nearly follows two lines of the figure. The forest covers an area of about twelve hundred square miles. It is a romantic seclusion, having Basle, Freiburg, and Baden-Baden for its cities of supply and exchange; full of pastoral richness, lonely grandeur; a land of fable and song.

The Black Forest Railway is one of the great triumphs of engineering skill. It is ninety-three miles long, and has some forty tunnels. It takes the traveller from Baden at once into the primeval solitudes. Freiburg, a very quaint town, is situated in the forest.

Master Lewis spoke briefly to the Club of Von Moltke, the great Prussian general.

MARSHAL VON MOLTKE.

Never was a nation more fortunate in its leaders than was Prussia when she aimed to achieve German unity. It is often the case that when some great crisis comes upon a country, men able to deal with it rise and become the guides of the people. This was never more true than it was of Prussia when, thirteen years ago, she entered upon the war with France which was to decide not only her own destiny, but that of the whole German people.

Three Prussians towered, at that time, far above the rest, — William, the wise and energetic king ; Bismarck, the resolute and far-seeing statesman ; and Von Moltke, the skilful and consummate soldier. It was the united action of these three, as much as the valor of the Prussian army, which not only won the victory, but gathered and garnered its fruits.

. All three of these men are still living (1882-83), and still active, each in his own sphere. The hale old king, now emperor, shows, at the age of eighty-six, little lessening of his sturdy powers. Bismarck, at seventy, still sways with his strong and stubborn will the affairs of the youthful empire. Von Moltke, at eighty-two, remains the foremost military figure of Germany.

Von Moltke is a very interesting personage. From his earliest youth he has followed the profession of arms. He has always been every inch a soldier. In the course of years, he became an absolute master of his art. He had military science at his fingers' ends. In every emergency he knew just what to do

To be sure, he has not been one of those brilliant and dashing military chiefs who, by their daring exploits and sudden triumphs, become heroes in the

VON MOLTKE.

eyes of men. He has been a careful, studious, deliberate commander, losing sight of nothing, ready for every exigency, looking well ahead, and closely calculating upon every possibility of events.

Yet the sturdy old soldier is by no means a dull man outside of his quarters or the barracks. In a quiet way, he enjoys life in many of its phases. He has always been a great reader on a great variety of subjects. He is known as one of the most delightful letter-writers in Germany. He is fond, too, of poetry, and reads history and fiction with much delight.

There is a Roman simplicity about Von Moltke's daily life. He lives in a building which serves as the headquarters of the general staff of the army in Berlin. Promptly at seven o'clock every morning, summer and winter, he enters his study, a plain room, with a table in the centre, covered with maps, papers, and books.

There he takes his coffee, at the same time smoking a cigar. He proceeds at once to work, and keeps at it till nine, when his mail is brought to him. At eleven he takes a plain breakfast, after which he again works steadily till two, when he holds a reception of officers.

The afternoon is devoted to work. After dinner, for the first time, this man of eighty-two enjoys some rest and recreation until eleven, at which hour he retires.

In personal appearance, Von Moltke is tall, thin, and slightly stooping. On horseback, however, he straightens up, and bears himself as erect as a man of thirty. His close-shaven face is much wrinkled, and his profile somewhat reminds one of that of Julius Cæsar. He never appears in any other than a military dress; and is often seen walking alone in the Thiergarten at Berlin, his hands clasped behind him and his head bent forward, after the manner of the great Napoleon.

Von Moltke married, some years ago, an English girl many years younger than himself. She died suddenly in 1868; and this event cast a shadow over all his later life. He has always since worn a sad and thoughtful face. He often visits his wife's grave in the country; and on the mausoleum which he erected to her memory, he has caused to be engraved the sentence, " Love is the fulfilling of the law."

The rest of the evening was spent in rehearsing Black Forest tales, one of the most interesting of which we give here.

SCRATCH GRAVEL; OR, THE ENCHANTED HEN.

Queer stories, as well as tragic ones, are related of the Black Forest; and one of the most popular legends of enchantment, the Hen Trench, is as absurd as it is amusing. Children like this story, for among German children the industrious and useful hen is something of a pet. Where, except in Germany, did there ever originate an heroic legend of a *hen?*

NIGHT SECOND. 99

The main line of the Baden railway runs southward towards Freiburg, amid some of the most picturesque mountain scenery of the Black Forest. The second station is Bühl, from which a delightful excursion may be made to Forbach and the Murg Valley.

Here may be seen the extensive ruins of the old castle of Windeck, which was destroyed in the year 1561, about which a very remarkable story is told.

The old lords of Windeck were very quarrelsome people. They had feud after feud with the neighboring lords, and were continually at war with the Prince Bishops of Strasburg.

Queer times were those, and queer relations existed between the Church and State. The Lord of Windeck was at one time kidnapped by the Bishop of Strasburg, and confined in a tower three years, — a thing that would not be regarded as a very clerical or spiritual proceeding to-day.

FOUNTAIN AT SCHAFFHAUSEN.

A little later the Dean of Strasburg was surprised by the retainers of the Lord of Windeck, and was in turn carried a prisoner to the gray old castle of Windeck.

The captive dean had a niece, a lovely girl, who was deeply attached to him. When she heard of his captivity she was much grieved, and set herself to devising plans for his release.

At the foot of the grim old castle, in the Black Forest, there lived an old woman. She was wiser than her neighbors, and was regarded as a witch. She was able to tell inquirers whatever they wished to know, and so was as useful as a newspaper, in her day and generation.

She was the last of her family. She lived alone, and her only society was some pure white hens, so large that the biggest of modern Shanghai fowls must have been mere pygmies to them.

The people of the region were very shy of the old woman and her strange hens. The timid never ventured past her door after dark, after her hens went to roost.

She was surprised one winter evening by a rap at her door.

She listened.

Tap, tap, tap!

"Come in."

A fair young girl lifted the latch.

"I am belated in the forest. Will you give me shelter?"

"Come in and sit down. Whence did you come?"

"I am on my way to the castle, but night has overtaken me."

"You are very near it. If it were light, I could show you its towers. But what can a dove like you be seeking in that vulture's nest?"

"My dear uncle, the Dean of Strasburg, is a prisoner there."

"I saw him when he was dragged into the castle, and very distressed and woe-begone the good man looked."

"I am going there to pray for his release."

"Umph. At that castle they don't give something for nothing. What ransom can you offer?"

"Nothing. I hope by prayers and tears to move the count's heart."

"I am wiser than you in the world's ways, — let me advise you. Cry with those pretty eyes, plead with your sweet voice, but not to the old count."

"To whom?"

"To his son."

"Will he influence his father?"

"Girl, I have taken a liking to you. You have a kind heart; I can see your disposition; I have met but few like you in the world. I will tell you what I will do. I will give you one of my white hens."

"A *hen?*"

"Yes. Go with the hen to the castle and inquire for Bernard, the count's son. Tell him that at daybreak the Count of Eberstein has planned an attack on the castle, and that you have come to warn him. Bid him fear nothing. Say that what he needs is a trench; and when he asks how one is to be made, tell

THE OLD WOMAN'S DIRECTIONS.

him that you have brought him Scratch Gravel, the hen, who will immediately dig one for him."

"How will that rescue my uncle?"

"You shall see."

The maiden took the white hen, and went out into the night. The old woman pointed out to her the way to the castle.

As she drew near the castle, she heard a great noise in the highway. The count's son was returning late from the chase. As he drew near her on horseback, he accosted her politely and asked her errand.

The beautiful girl related the story the old woman had told her.

"I will take you to my father."

She related her story to the count, and showed him the white hen.

"Pooh! pooh!" said the count.

"I think her story is true," said the young man.

"Why?"

"I see truth written on her beautiful face."

"Is that so? I don't see it. Perhaps my eyes are not as good as they used to be. Well, well; let us see what the white hen will do."

They took the hen outside the castle, and put her down. Presently the gravel began to fly. It was like a storm. The air was filled with earth and stones, and the old count was filled with astonishment.

"The hen is bewitched," said the count.

"Did I not tell you that the girl is honest?"

"And handsome?"

"And handsome."

Before daybreak the white hen had dug a deep trench around the castle. The trench is shown to travellers to-day, a very remarkable proof of the truth of the story, with only one missing link in the chain of evidence.

The next morning the enemy appeared, but when he came to the trench he forbore to storm the castle.

The old count called the maiden into his presence.

"What reward do you ask for so great a service?"

"That you call the Dean of Strasburg to give thanks in the chapel."

The count called the bishop, and attended the service. When it was over, he did not remand the good man to his cell.

"I have one request to make of you," said Bernard to the maid, as they left the church.

"Name it."

"You promise to grant it?"

"Name it."

"That you make your home in the castle."

"On one condition."

"Name it."

"That the dean is released."

The young count went to his father.

"The maiden has one request to make."

"She shall have her request."

So the dean was released and went back to Strasburg. The maid became the wife of the young count, but what became of the hen the chroniclers do not tell.

But the trench remains, — the *Henne-Graben*, — and all that is wanting to make the evidence of the story sure is to connect the hen with the trench, after four hundred years. This may not be hard; geologists make connections in like cases after the lapse of a thousand years. Do they not?

CHAPTER VII.

EVENING THE THIRD.

STRASBURG. — A MEMORABLE CHRISTMAS. — THE STORY OF THE LOST ORGANIST.

UR third night upon the Rhine was spent at Strasburg.
"The cathedral is the wonder of the city. The excursionist thinks of but little else during his stay there. Wherever he may be, the gigantic church is always in view. He beholds it towering over all.

"Its history is that of Germany. It grew with the German empire, and has shared all its triumphs and reverses. It was founded by Clovis. It has been imperilled by lightning some fifty times, and has as often repelled the shocks of war. In the tenth century it was burned; in the eleventh, plundered; and five years after it was nearly demolished by lightning.

"It was after the last calamity that the present structure was begun. At one time a *hundred thousand* men were employed upon it: can we wonder that it is colossal?

"The giant grew. In 1140, 1150, and 1176 it was partly burned, but it rose from the flames always more great, lofty, and splendid.

"Indulgences were offered to donors and workmen; to contributors of all kinds. Men earned, or thought they earned, their salvation by adding their mites to the spreading magnificence. In 1303 it is said that all the peasants of Alsace might be seen drawing stone into Stras-

STRASBURG CATHEDRAL

burg for the cathedral. Master builder succeeded master builder, — died, — but the great work went on. In the French Revolution the Jacobins tore from the cathedral the statues of two hundred and thirty saints; but it was still a city of saints in stone and marble. In 1870, in the Franco-Prussian war, its roof was perforated with shells, and on

PLATFORM OF STRASBURG CATHEDRAL.

the 25th of August it burst into flames, and it was telegraphed over the world that the great cathedral was destroyed. But it stands to-day, majestic, regal, and beautiful, its spire piercing the sky.

"We visited the cathedral in the afternoon. We were at once filled with wonder at the windows. They burned with color, and seemed to hang in air amid the shadows of the lofty walls. They represented scriptural subjects.

"I was standing in awe, gazing upon a gorgeous circular window that seemed to blaze in the air like a planet, when Charlie touched my arm.

"'The clock?'

"'What?'

"'Can we not go up and see the fixings, and how it is all done?'

"'I am not thinking of that *toy*,' said I; 'you stand in a monument of art that it has taken a thousand years to build.'

"'Yes; I hope we shall be here to-morrow when the Twelve Apostles come out and the cock crows *at* Peter.'"

A MEMORABLE CHRISTMAS.

The soldiers of Aurelian, the Roman emperor, used to sing, —

"We have slain a thousand Franks."

"We have cut off the heads of a thousand, thousand, thousand, thousand.
One man hath cut off the heads of a thousand, thousand, thousand, thousand, thousand;
May he live a thousand years."

The Franks came out of the North, and established themselves in Gaul and Germania during the period of the early Roman emperors. Their most renowned king was Clovis, with whom began the empire of France. He was a savage and passionate man, born to command and to conquer. He was a heathen. It is related of him that once, when he had enriched himself with spoils from some of the early Christian churches, the Bishop of Rheims desired that he would return a valued vase that had been taken from the cathedral.

"Follow us to Soissons," said Clovis; "there the booty will be divided."

In the division of the booty, a high-spirited and selfish Frankish chieftain objected to the bishop's claim, and, to show his contempt for him and the Church, struck the vase with his battle-axe. Clovis was offended. He gave the bishop the vase, and soon after avenged the insult by striking the chieftain dead with his own battle-axe, saying, —

"Thus didst thou to the vase at Soissons."

His wife, Clotilde, was a Christian, and she often tried to persuade him to embrace the Christian faith.

In 496 the Allemannians, a German confederation, who had been assailing the Roman colonies on the Rhine, crossed the river, and invaded the territory of the Franks. Clovis met the invaders near Cologne. A severe battle followed. Clovis was hard pressed.

THUS DIDST THOU TO THE VASE OF SOISSONS.

He called upon his gods, but they did not answer him. He saw he was in danger of being utterly defeated and losing his army.

He had with him a servant of the queen.

"My Lord King," said this man, "believe only on the Lord of heaven, whom the queen, my mistress, preacheth."

Clovis raised his eyes in hope towards heaven, —

"Christ Jesus, thou whom my queen Clotilde calleth the Son of God, I have called upon my own gods, and they have left me. Thee I invoke. Give me victory, and I will believe in thee, proclaim thee to my people, and be baptized in thy name."

The tide of battle now suddenly turned, the Allemannians were beaten, and their king was slain.

When his queen had learned of his vow, she sent for the Bishop of Rheims to instruct him in Christianity. He publicly renounced his gods, and his people at the same time accepted the queen's faith.

STREET IN STRASBURG.

Christmas Day, 496, will be ever memorable in Christian history; it was on that day that the King of the Franks was baptized.

The occasion was one of barbaric splendor, and such as might be expected of a warlike king in those rude times. The road from the palace to the baptistery, over which the king was to pass, was curtained with silk, mottoes, and banners, like a triumphal way. The houses of Rheims were hung with festive ornaments, and the baptistery itself was sprinkled with balm and "all manner of perfume."

The procession moved from the palace like a pageant for a feast of victory. The clergy led, bearing the Gospels, standards, and cross. Hymns were chanted, as they swept along. Then came the Bishop of Rheims, leading the king; after him, the rejoicing queen; and lastly the neophytes who were to receive baptism with the king.

On the way, the king seemed impressed with the glittering pageant.

"Is this kingdom promised me?" he asked.

"No," said the bishop; "but it is the entrance to the road that leads to it."

At the baptistery the bishop said to the king, —

"Lower your head with humility; adore what thou hast burned; burn what thou hast adored."

Clovis was then solemnly baptized, and with him three thousand warriors. With the imposing rite, Christianity in France began, and with him began that great monument of the faith, Strasburg Cathedral.

Charley Leland furnished the most interesting story on this evening. It well illustrated features of German and French musical life that are unknown in America. In Germany and in the French provinces the organist of the town is a very important person. The choice of an organist in these towns is a very interesting event, and during the last century excited more discussion than at the present time.

THE YOUNG ORGANIST: A MYSTERY.

The towns on the Rhine are all famous for their organs, and proud of the eminent organists they have had in the past. Each town points with pride to some musical legend and history.

The story I have to tell is associated with an ancient provincial town.

It is now hardly more than a small town, and possesses not above a thousand inhabitants; but in the latter part of the last century it was more than ten times

CLOVIS

its present size, and its church, now in ruins, was then one of the most beautiful ever seen in that part of the country.

This church was finished in the year 1795, and was for a long time the great object of curiosity for miles around. It was of the Gothic and Romanesque style of architecture, and was not only finely proportioned on the exterior, but had within a magnificence of decoration that astonished one more and more the longer he gazed upon it.

The church, unlike some of the older ones standing at that time, had a magnificent organ. This had been paid for by a separate subscription, raised in small sums by the common people, and, having been built by skilful workmen in Bordeaux, was at length set up in the church amid considerable enthusiasm and excitement.

But who should play this grand instrument? How should a competent organist be selected?

The people were greatly interested in the matter, and discussed it on the corner of the *rues*, in the *brasseries* or taverns ; and for a period of six or eight weeks you might be sure, if you saw more than two people talking earnestly together, that they were deliberating upon the choice of an organist.

Since the people, both high and low, had so freely contributed for the purchase of the organ, it was thought very proper that they should be allowed to choose a person to play it. And, the decision being thus left to the multitude, the most feasible plan that was suggested was that all should go, on an appointed day, to the church, and should then listen to the playing of the various candidates.

There were, in all, nearly a score of aspiring musicians in and near the town ; and each of these, hoping for a favorable decision for himself, gave no end of little suppers and parties, so that the influential ones among the townsmen fared sumptuously from all.

But out of the entire number there were two, between whom the choice really lay. These were Baptiste Lacombe and Raoul Tegot.

The former of these had lived in the town only five years. He had come from Bruges, so he said ; and although he astonished everybody by his skill, he had not been liked from the first. He was very reserved and parsimonious, and his eye never met frankly the person with whom he talked. But no harm was known of him, and he found in Tranteigue plenty of exercise for his art.

Raoul Tegot, on the contrary, was a native of the town ; and, together with his young son, François, was beloved by all. He had married one of the village maidens, and had been so inconsolable at her death, which occurred when François was a baby, that he never thought more of marriage, but devoted himself to his child and his art.

He was certainly a very able musician, and, being so universally liked, many people urged that a public performance be dispensed with, and that he be elected at once. But although Baptiste Lacombe was not *liked*, his *skill* found many admirers; and, besides, it was flattering to the worthy country-folk to think of sitting solemnly in judgment at the great church; and so the proposed plan was adhered to.

Finally, the weeks of anticipation came to an end, the appointed day was at hand, and, according to the arrangements previously made, at nine o'clock in the forenoon the three great doors of the church were swung open, and the throng, orderly and even dignified, entered and filled the edifice.

The seats, which in French churches and cathedrals are movable, had all been taken away, and the crowd quite filled the whole space. All male inhabitants of the town who were over twenty years of age were to vote, and each, the town officials and the poorest artisans alike, had one ballot.

The great and beautiful organ took up nearly the whole of the large gallery over the entrance, and extended up and up into the clear-story until it was mingled with the supports of the roof.

In the organ-loft the candidates were crowded together in eager expectation, and the glances that passed from one to another were not the kindliest. Each of them had been allowed several hours, at some time during the past week, for practice on the instrument; and each doubtless considered himself deserving of the position.

Presently, when all was still, Monseigneur Jules Émile Gautier, a very learned gentleman of the town, who had been chosen for that purpose, ascended two steps of the stairway which curved up and around the richly carved pulpit, and announced the name of the person who was to begin.

I should not be able to give, in detail, the progress of the trial; for the history of the affair is not minute enough for that. But suffice it to say that the last name on the list was Raoul Tegot; and the name immediately preceding it was that of Baptiste Lacombe.

At length, in his turn, Monsieur Lacombe, his iron-gray hair disordered, his hands rubbing together nervously, and his eyes flashing — as was afterwards remarked upon — with a malicious fire, stepped forward and along to the organ-seat, and for a few moments arranged his stops.

Then he began lightly and delicately, creeping up through the varied registers of the noble instrument, blending the beautiful sounds into wonderful combinations, now and then working in a sweet melody, and then again upward until the grand harmonies of the full organ rolled forth. There was something mysterious and awe-inspiring in the effort. It seemed to the people that they had never heard music before.

The music ceased. The people came back to their prosaic selves again, looked in each other's faces, and said, with one breath, "Wonderful!"

Gradually they recovered their sober judgment, and then, mingled with the murmurs of admiration, were heard the remarks, "That is fine, but Raoul Tegot will make us forget it!" "Yes, wait until you hear Raoul Tegot!"

Soon Gautier ascended the two steps of the pulpit, and called the name of their kind, generous townsman.

All waited breathlessly. All eyes were turned towards the organ-loft. The musicians there looked around and at each other. But poor Raoul Tegot could not be seen.

Where was he? The people waited and wondered, but he did not come. Monsieur Baptiste Lacombe was greatly excited, and was wiping the perspiration from his heated face. "Perhaps he was afraid to come," he ventured to remark to a man near him, at the same time looking out of a window.

Several noticed his agitation; but they only said, "Ah, mon Dieu, how he did play! No wonder that he is nervous."

The disquiet and confusion in the nave and aisles increased.

A messenger had been sent to look for the missing man; but he could not be found.

What was to be done?

Finally, some friends of Monsieur Lacombe made bold to urge his immediate election, declaring that he had far surpassed all competitors; and they even hinted at cowardice on the part of Raoul Tegot.

This insinuation was indignantly denied by Tegot's friends, who were very numerous but helpless; they knew their friend too well to believe him capable of such conduct. He was, they said, probably detained somewhere by an accident.

But, wherever he was, he was *not* present; and when a vote was taken, hastily, by a showing of hands, Monsieur Baptiste Lacombe had ten times as many ballots as any other person, and, of course, poor Monsieur Tegot, not having competed, was not balloted for at all.

The people dispersed to their homes; some in vexation that their favorite had not appeared, others in a little alarm at his strange absence. Young François Tegot had not seen his father since early morning, and could not conjecture where he might be.

The next day the missing organist did not appear, and his friends began to inquire and to search for him; but they were wholly unsuccessful. A little boy said that he had seen him go into the church with Monsieur Lacombe early that morning; but Monsieur Lacombe said, very distinctly and with some vehemence, that the missing man had left the church an hour later to go to a cottage at the edge of the town, where he was to give a lesson in singing.

So the affair lay wrapped in mystery. There were many surmises, but nothing definite was known. A few expressed suspicion of the rival candidate; but the suspicion was too great to be thrown rashly upon anybody. Thus no progress in the inquiry was made. A human life did not mean so much in those stormy days after the Revolution as formerly; and the mysterious disappearance, without being in the least cleared up, gradually faded from men's minds and passed out of their conversation.

Months and years passed away, and nothing was known of the poor man. His son, now come to the years of manhood, always declared that his father would not have been absent from the trial willingly; and he firmly believed that he had met with a violent death. More than this he would not say; but sometimes when he looked towards Monsieur Baptiste Lacombe, — still the respected organist of the church, — his eyes were observed to flash meaningly.

There was to be a grand *fête* in the church, and great preparation was made. As the organ needed repairs, it was decided to repair it thoroughly; and one of the builders from Bordeaux was sent for.

He was to come on Thursday; but he chanced to arrive the day before, and was to begin work early the following morning. That night a light glimmered out of the darkness of the gallery of the church.

Two days passed. The repairing of the organ went on; but there was much to be done, and it might take a week. One afternoon, as François passed through the centre of the village, two men came hurriedly out of the town-house, and hastened away towards the church. It was the organ-builder, very much excited, and one of the officials of the town. The young man, venturing on his well-known skill as an organist, followed them; and the three entered the building. A few worshippers were at the great altar, and the sacred edifice seemed unusually quiet and peaceful.

The organ-builder seemed too agitated to answer the questions that the town official asked him, but led the way quickly to the organ-loft. "Put your foot on that pedal!" he said excitedly, pointing to a particular one of the scale.

The official was too bewildered to comply, and François did it for him.

"Now try the next one!" said he.

François did so, but no sound came; only a queer, intermittent rumbling, like a bounding and rebounding.

"It does not sound," said the organ-builder. "Follow me and I will show you why."

"It never has sounded since the great trial-day, years ago," muttered the young man. But he followed on.

They clambered up a rickety staircase, a still more rickety ladder, and came to a platform at a level with the top of the organ; and all around them, reaching up out of the dim light below, were the open pipes. Passing hurriedly around, on a narrow plank, to the back of the organ, their agitated guide paused before a row of immense pedal pipes, and, without allowing his own eyes to look, he held the light that he carried for the others.

Both looked down into the cavernous tube that he indicated, and both started back in surprise and fear.

"It is a man's legs!" gasped the frightened town official.

After the first moment of surprise had passed, they began to get back their wits; and the young man advised that they send for several strong men and lift out the pipe.

This seemed sensible, and in a half-hour the men were at hand and the pipe was drawn down to the level of the organ-loft and laid horizontally. The work-

men had been informed of the nature of their work, and all were under intense excitement. The pipe was very long, and the body was at least five feet from the top. One of the workmen reached in a pole having a hook at the end, and the next minute drew forth the dead body of the sinister old organist, Baptiste Lacombe.

There was a pause of silent horror. Nobody cared particularly for the dead man, but the manner of his death was terrible.

"How did it happen?" whispered one.

"Perhaps it was suicide," answered another.

They began more closely to examine the huge tube. François Tegot, who, although thus far cooler than the others, now seemed unable to stand, pointed to the hand of the dead man, which was tightly clenched upon a small cord. One of the workmen approached, and with some difficulty drew out the line; and a new thrill of expectation went through the silent company when they saw, attached to the end of the line, an old leather bundle covered with dust.

Young Tegot now seemed to master himself by a great effort, and, motioning the workman back, he advanced, and, lifting the bag tenderly out into a more convenient position, he said solemnly, as if to himself, "I have long suspected something was wrong, and now I shall know."

Then he examined the bag, and at length took from his pocket a knife and carefully cut open one side.

Despite the fact that he expected the revelation that now came, he started back, for the opening revealed a piece of cloth,—a coat, which even the town official could recollect to be the coat of the long-lost organist, Raoul Tegot, François's father.

The young man stepped back and sank again into his seat, and the others, coming forward, laid the bag quite open, and drew forth a watch and an embroidered vest; in a pocket of the coat was found a purse. "Here is an odd treasure," said one of the workmen, holding up a locket of dull gold.

François seized it and opened it. The color forsook his face and his eyes filled with tears. He simply said,—

"My mother."

The town official now whispered to the surprised organ-builder, that the villanous Lacombe had killed poor Tegot on the morning of the trial, and had secreted the body in some unknown place and hidden the valuables here. Frightened by the fear of discovery, he had attempted to remove the treasures, had fallen into the pipe, and had thus met a horrible death.

"There is nothing secret," said François, "but shall be revealed. Sin is its own detector, and its secrets cannot rest."

The excitement among the townspeople was for many days even greater than it had been at the time of Tegot's disappearance, and many and bitter were the reproaches heaped upon the wicked organist's memory.

François was immediately chosen organist, and held the position during his entire life.

CHAPTER VIII.

EVENING THE FOURTH.

SEVEN NIGHTS ON THE RHINE: — HEIDELBERG. — STUDENTS. — STUDENT SONGS. — THE STORY OF LITTLE MOOK. — THE QUEER OLD LADY WHO WENT TO COLLEGE.

EIDELBERG," said Mr. Beal, "stands bright and clear beside Neckar, a branch of the Rhine, as though it loved the river. It is semicircled with blue mountain-walls, and is full of balmy air and cheerful faces. The streets have an atmosphere of hospitality. Its history dates from the Roman monuments on its hills, and is associated with the romantic times of the counts-palatine of the Rhine.

"The world-wide fame of Heidelberg arises from its university. This was founded in 1386, and is the oldest in Germany. It made Heidelberg a student-town; there art flourished and free thought grew, and it became the gem of German cities.

"The ancient Castle of Heidelberg is one of the wonders of Germany. It is like a ruined town of palaces, and historic and poetic associations are as thick as are the violets among its ruins. It is said that Michael Angelo designed it: we cannot tell. The names of the masters who upreared the pile of magnificence for centuries and peopled it with statues are lost. The ivy creeps over their conceptions in stone and marble, and the traveller exclaims in awe, 'Can it be that all this glory was created for destruction?'

"We visited the castle at noon. A ruin green with ivy rose before

PALACE AT HEIDELBERG.

us. The sunlight fell through the open doorways, and the swallows flitted in and out of the window-frames into roofless chambers.

"I was dreaming of the past: of the counts-palatine of the Rhine, of stately dames, orange-gardens, and splendid festivals, when one of the boys recalled my thoughts to the present.

"'Where is the tun?'

"'What tun?'

"'The one *we have come to see*,—the big wine-cask. It is said to hold two hundred and thirty-six thousand bottles of wine, or did in the days of the nobles.'

"'I remember: when I was a boy my mental picture of Heidelberg was a big wine-cask.'

"'Yes; well, please, sir, I am a boy now.'"

Mr. Beal then gave a brief account of

GERMAN STUDENT LIFE.

The town of Heidelberg nestles in one of the loveliest valleys in Europe. The Neckar winds between a series of steep, high, thickly wooded hills.

It is amid such pleasant scenes that the famous university is situated, and that several hundred German students are gathered to pursue their studies.

One of my chief objects in visiting Heidelberg was to see the university, and to observe the curious student customs of which I had heard so much; and my journey was amply repaid by what I saw.

The university itself was far less imposing than I had imagined; compared with the picturesque and hoary old college palaces of Oxford and Cambridge, or even with our own cosey Harvard and Yale edifices and greens, it seemed very insignificant.

The buildings occupy a cheerless square in a central part of the quaint old German town. They are very plain, modest, and unpretending. The lecture-rooms are on one side of the square; in the rear are the museum and reading room, while opposite the lecture-rooms is a row of jewelry, clothing, confectionery, and other shops. I was most interested, however, in the students and their ways.

As soon as you enter the town and pass up the main street, you espy groups of the students here and there. You are at once struck with the contrast they present to American or English students. Very odd to American eyes are their dress and manners. Let me describe one to you as an example.

THE GERMAN STUDENT.

The Heidelberg student is a rather large, heavy-looking fellow, with round face, broad shoulders, and a very awkward gait. His hair is cropped close to his head, and on one side of the head, in jaunty fashion, he wears a small round cap, — too small by far to cover it, as caps generally do. It is of red or blue or green, and worked with fanciful figures of gold or silver thread.

GERMAN STUDENT.

On his feet are heavy boots, which rise, outside his trousers, nearly to the knees. His body is covered with a gay frock-coat, of green or gray or black. As he walks the street with his college mates, he puffs away on a very curious long pipe, the bowl being of porcelain, on which is painted some fanciful scene, or perhaps a view of the grand old castle. Sometimes the stem of the pipe is two or three feet long. In his hand he carries a cane, or rather stick (for it is too short to be used as a cane), with some curiously carved figure for a handle.

Many of the Heidelberg students are attended, wherever they go, by a companion who is apt to produce fear and dislike in those who are not accustomed to him. This is a small, blear-eyed, bullet-headed, bloodthirsty-looking bull-dog, with red eyes and snarling mouth. You see such dogs everywhere with the students, running close to their heels, and ready, at an instant's notice, to defend their masters.

CASTLE AT HEIDELBERG

Almost every Heidelberg student belongs to one of the social societies, of which some are called "Verbindungs," and others "Corps;" and the caps they wear designate the particular societies of which they are members.

These societies are both patriotic and social. The members devote themselves to "the glory of the Fatherland;" and they pledge themselves by oaths to defend and aid each other.

Besides the cap, the students betray to what society they belong by various colored ribbons across their breasts or hung to their watch-chains. There is a great deal of rivalry among the societies, which results in frequent difficulties.

The pastimes of the Heidelberg students are almost entirely confined to the "good times" they have in their "Verbindungs," in which they meet two nights in the week to sing, make funny speeches, and perform certain curious ceremonies.

The students often make excursions to a beautiful spot on the Neckar, called "Wolfsbrunnen," where they obtain trout fresh from a pond, and eat them, nicely cooked, on tables set out under the trees near the river-side.

Another frequent recreation is to attend the peasant fairs in the neighboring villages, and to take jaunts to the lovely Swetzingen gardens, or to the top of the Konigsthul hill, back of the castle, from which a most beautiful view of the Black Forest and Hartz Mountains, with the broad valley of the Rhine, is to be seen.

On this hill is an inn where many resort to drink whey. Many of the students are too poor to enjoy the pastimes of the others, or even to live at the university without doing something to support themselves.

These go wandering about the country in vacation time, on foot, singing in the villages, and receiving money from the kindly disposed, with which to pay the expenses of their education. As you pass through Germany you frequently meet parties of these poor students, who go about merrily; and to give them a few kreuzers is always a pleasure.

Mr. Beal gave from translations a few specimens of these German student songs. The first was

GAUDEAMUS.

Let us then rejoice, ere youth
From our grasp hath hurried;
After cheerful youth is past,
After cheerless age, at last,
In the earth we 're buried.

Where are those who lived of yore,
  Men whose days are over?
To the realms above thee go,
Thence unto the shades below,
  An' thou wilt discover.

Short and fleeting is our life, —
  Swift away 't is wearing;
Swiftly, too, will death be here,
Cruel, us away to tear,
  Naught that liveth sparing.

Long live Academia, —
  And our tutors clever;
All our comrades long live they,
And our female comrades gay,
  May they bloom forever.

Long live every maiden true,
  Who has worth and beauty;
And may every matron who
Kind and good is, flourish, too, —
  Each who does her duty.

Long may also live our state,
  And the king who guides us;
Long may live our town, and fate
Prosper each Mecænas great,
  Who good things provides us.

Perish melancholy woe,
  Perish who derides us;
Perish fiend, and perish so
Every antiburschian foe
  Who for laughing chides us.

Mr. Beal, finding the Class interested, continued the subject by some account of one of the most popular writers of German songs.

HEINE.

The songs of Heine are unmatched in German literature, and have been translated into all European tongues. Their beauty of expression, and sugges-

GERMAN STUDENTS.

tive and evasive meanings, have made them household words in Germany, and favorite quotations in France and England.

The career of Heine was exceptionably brilliant, and he won tributes of admiration that have seldom been equalled. It is said that on the appearance of his "Reisebilder" in 1826-31, "young Germany became intoxicated with enthusiasm." His writings on republicanism not only won the heart of the people, but carried his influence into other countries.

From his youth Heine was troubled by thoughts of personal religious responsibility. There were periods when he earnestly sought to know man's true relations to God. He sought the evidence of truth, however, more from nature, philosophy, and history, than by the prayers and the faith which God's Word inculcates.

He was born a Jew, but abandoned Judaism and was baptized in the Lutheran Church. Then he became a free-thinker. He studied various philosophies and systems of belief, but was not able to arrive at any satisfactory conclusions.

In 1847 he was attacked by a strange disease. It paralyzed his body, and confined him for many years to his chair. For seven years he was propped up by pillows, and read his praises on a couch of suffering, and they made his life more sad.

"What good," he said, in despair, "does it do me to hear that my health is drunk in cups of gold, when I can only wet my lips with barley-water?"

In this condition he read "Uncle Tom's Cabin." It revealed to him the truth that religion is a matter of experience rather than philosophy, and that the humblest may receive the evidence of its truth through simple faith in Christ.

"With all my learning," he said, "the poor negro knew more about religion than I do now, and I must come to a knowledge of the truth in the same humble way as poor Uncle Tom."

He left this testimony in his will: "I have cast aside all philosophical pride, and have again felt the power of religious truth."

I will recite to you one of the songs of Heine, which is popular among the German students.

THE LORELEI.

I know not whence it rises,
This thought so full of woe;
But a tale of times departed
Haunts me, and will not go.

The air is cool, and it darkens,
   And calmly flows the Rhine;
The mountain-peaks are sparkling
   In the sunny evening-shine.

And yonder sits a maiden,
   The fairest of the fair;
With gold is her garment glittering,
   And she combs her golden hair:

With a golden comb she combs it;
   And a wild song singeth she,
That melts the heart with a wondrous
   And powerful melody.

The boatman feels his bosom
   With a nameless longing move;
He sees not the gulfs before him,
   His gaze is fixed above,

Till over boat and boatman
   The Rhine's deep waters run:
And this, with her magic singing,
   The Lorelei has done!

Among the pleasing stories related on this evening was "Little Mook," by Hauff, and a poetic account of a "Queer Old Lady who went to College."

LITTLE MOOK.

There once lived a dwarf in the town of Niceu, whom the people called Little Mook. He lived alone, and was thought to be rich. He had a very small body and a very large head, and he wore an enormous turban.

He seldom went into the streets, for the reason that ill-bred children there followed and annoyed him. They used to cry after him, —

"Little Mook, O Little Mook,
   Turn, oh, turn about and look!
Once a month you leave your room,
   With your head like a balloon:
Try to catch us, if you can;
   Turn and look, my little man."

ENTRANCE TO HEIDELBERG CASTLE.

I will tell you his history.

His father was a hard-hearted man, and treated him unkindly because he was deformed. The old man at last died, and his relatives drove the dwarf away from his home.

He wandered into the strange world with a cheerful spirit, for the strange world was more kind to him than his kin had been.

He came at last to a strange town, and looked around for some face that should seem pitiful and friendly. He saw an old house, into whose door a great number of cats were passing. "If the people here are so good to cats, they may be kind to me," he thought, and so he followed them. He was met by an old woman, who asked him what he wanted.

He told his sad story.

"I don't cook any but for my darling pussy cats," said the beldame ; "but I pity your hard lot, and you may make your home with me until you can find a better."

So Little Mook was employed to look after the cats and kittens.

LITTLE MOOK.

The kittens, I am sorry to say, used to behave very badly when the old dame went abroad ; and when she came home and found the house in confusion, and bowls and vases broken, she used to berate Little Mook for what he could not help.

While in the old lady's service he discovered a secret room in which were magic articles, among them a pair of enormous slippers.

One day when the old lady was out the little dog broke a crystal vase. Little Mook knew that he would be held responsible for the accident, and he resolved to escape and try his fortune in the world again. He would need good shoes, for the journey might be long ; so he put on the big slippers and ran away.

Ran? What wonderful slippers those were! He had only to say to them, "Go!" and they would impel him forward with the rapidity of the wind. They seemed to him like wings.

"I will become a courier," said Little Mook, "and so make my fortune, sure." So Little Mook went to the palace in order to apply to the king.

He first met the messenger-in-ordinary.

"What!" said he, "you want to be the king's messenger, — you with your little feet and great slippers!"

"Will you allow me to make a trial of speed with your swiftest runner?" asked Little Mook.

The messenger-in-ordinary told the king about the little man and his application.

"We will have some fun with him," said the king. "Let him run a race with my first messenger for the sport of the court."

So it was arranged that Little Mook should try his speed with the swiftest messenger.

Now the king's runner was a very tall man. His legs were very long and slender; he had little flesh on his body. He walked with wonderful swiftness, looking like a windmill as he strode forward. He was the telegraph of his times, and the king was very proud of him.

The next day the king, who loved a jest, summoned his court to a meadow to witness the race, and to see what the bumptious pygmy could do. Everybody was on tiptoe of expectation, being sure that something amusing would follow.

When Little Mook appeared he bowed to the spectators, who laughed at him. When the signal was given for the two to start, Little Mook allowed the runner to go ahead of him for a little time, but when the latter drew near the king's seat he passed him, to the wonder of all the people, and easily won the race.

The king was delighted, the princess waved her veil, and the people all shouted, "Huzza for Little Mook!"

So Little Mook became the royal messenger, and surpassed all the runners in the world with his magic slippers.

But Little Mook's great success with his magic slippers excited envy, and made him bitter enemies, and at last the king himself came to believe the stories of his enemies, and turned against him and banished him from his kingdom.

Little Mook wandered away, sore at heart, and as friendless as when he had left home and the house of the old woman. Just beyond the confines of the kingdom he came to a grove of fig-trees full of fruit.

He stopped to rest and refresh himself with the fruit. There were two trees that bore the finest figs he had ever seen. He gathered some figs from one of them, but as he was eating them his nose and ears began to *grow*, and when he looked down into a clear, pure stream near by, he saw that his head had been changed into a head like a donkey.

He sat down under the *other* fig-tree in despair. At last he took up a fig that had fallen from this tree, and ate it. Immediately his nose and ears became smaller and smaller and resumed their natural shape. Then he perceived that the trees bore magic fruit.

"Happy thought!" said Little Mook. "I will go back to the palace and sell the fruit of the first tree to the royal household, and then I will turn doctor, and give the donkeys the fruit of the second tree as medicine. But I will not give the old king any medicine."

Little Mook gathered the two kinds of figs, and returned to the palace and sold that of the first tree to the butler.

Oh, then there was woe in the palace! The king's family were seen wandering around with donkeys' heads on their shoulders. Their noses and ears were as long as their arms. The physicians were sent for and they held a *consultation*. They decided on amputation; but as fast as they cut off the noses and ears of the afflicted household, these troublesome members grew out again, longer than before.

Then Little Mook appeared with the principles and remedies of homœopathy. He gave one by one of the sufferers the figs of the *second* tree, and they were cured. He collected his fees, and having relieved all but the king he fled, taking his homœopathic arts with him. The king wore the head of a donkey to his latest day.

THE QUEER OLD LADY WHO WENT TO COLLEGE.

There was a queer old lady, and she had lost her youth;
  She bought her a new mirror,
And it told to her the truth.
   Did she break the truthful mirror?
     Oh, no, no; no, no, no, no.

But she bought some stays quite rare,
Some false teeth and wavy hair,
Some convex-concave glasses such as men of culture wear,
And then she looked again,
And she said, "I am not plain, —
I am not plain, 't is plain,
Not very, very plain,
I did not think that primps and crimps
Would change a body so.
I 'll take a book on Art,
And press it to my heart,
And I 'll straightway go to college,
Where I think I 'll catch a beau."

"And it told to her the truth."

II.

She made her way to college just as straight as straight could be,
And she asked for the Professor of the new philosophie;
He met her with a smile
And said, "Pray rest awhile,
And come into my parlor and take a cup of tea.
We will talk of themes celestial, —
Of the flowery nights in June
When blow the gentle zephyrs;
Of the circle round the moon;
Of the causes of the causes."
These college men are quite and very much polite,
And when you call upon them they you straightway in invite.

"Not very, very plain."

III.

But the lady she was modest,
    And she said, "You me confuse;
I have come, O man of wisdom,
    To get a bit of news.
There 's a problem of life's problems
    That often puzzles me:
Tell me true, O man of Science,
    When my wedding-day will be."

IV.

Quick by the hand he seized her,
    He of the philosophie,
And his answer greatly pleased her
    When they had taken tea:
"'T will be, my fair young lady,
    When you are *twenty-three!*"

"They you straightway in invite."

V.

At her window, filled with flowers,
Then she waited happy hours,
Scanned the byways and the highways
  To see what she could see.
If the postman brought a letter,
It was sure to greatly fret her, —
Fret her so her maid she 'd frighten,
  If a dun it proved to be.
If it came not from a lover,
Sadly she her face would cover,
Hide her face and say in sorrow,
" Truly *he* will come to-morrow,
For he knew, that man of science,
  And I 'm *almost* twenty-three."

VI.

He deceived her, he deceived her,
Oh, that too kind man deceived her, —
He of compasses and lenses,
He of new-found influences,
  He of the philosophie.
Oh the chatterer, oh the flatterer,
Oh the smatterer in science,
  To whom all things clear should be !
Had he taken the old almanac,
That true guide to worldly wisdom,
He would have seen that there was something —
Some stray figure, some lost factor,
Something added the extractor —
  Wrong in his chronologie,
  In his learned chronologie.

MORAL.

There are few things, one, two, three,
In the earth, the air, and sea,
That the schoolmen do not know.
When you 're going to catch a beau,
And a few like occultations,
  In a few things here below,
  Men of wisdom do not know ;
And to them for these few items
  It is never wise to go.

"HE OF THE PHILOSOPHIE."

CHAPTER IX.

FIFTH MEETING FOR RHINE STORIES.

SEVEN NIGHTS ON THE RHINE: — WORMS. — LUTHER'S MONUMENT. — THE STORY OF SIEGFRIED AND THE DRAGON. — MAYENCE. — BOAT JOURNEY. — STORIES OF THE CASTLES ON THE MIDDLE RHINE. — THE WONDERFUL STORY OF THE LORELEI. — KERNER.

R. BEAL continued the narrative of travel at the fifth meeting of the Club for the rehearsal of Rhine stories.

"We passed over a road along the right bank of the Rhine towards Worms. We journeyed amid green forests, and past fields which had heaped up harvests for a thousand years. Spires gleamed on the opposite bank, and in the flat landscape Worms came to view, the Rhine flowing calmly by.

"We stopped at Worms to see the cathedral and the Luther Monument. It is a dull town. We recalled that it was here great Cæsar stood, and Attila drove his cavalry of devastation over the Rhine. Here lived the hero of German classic song, — Siegfried. The cathedral has a monumental history. In 772 war was declared in it against the Saxons. Here was held the famous Diet of Worms at which Luther appeared, and said, —

"'Here I stand; I cannot do otherwise. God help me.'

"The cathedral is of the style called Romanesque. It is lofty and gloomy. Worms itself is a shadowy and silent city as compared with the past.

"The Luther Monument is a history of Protestantism in stone and bronze. It is one of the noblest works of art of modern times, and its majesty and unity are a surprise to the traveller. Luther is of course the central figure. He stands with his Bible in his hands, and his face upturned to heaven. Around him are the figures of the great reformers before the Reformation: Wycliffe, of England; Waldo, of

A BATTLE BETWEEN FRANKS AND SAXONS.

France; Huss, of Bohemia; and Savonarola, of Italy. The German princes who befriended and sustained the Reformer occupy conspicuous places, and the immense group presents a most impressive scene, associated with lofty character and commanding talent.

"We went to the place where Luther sat beneath a tree, when his companions sought to dissuade him from entering Worms.

"'I would go to Worms,' he said, 'were there as many devils as there are tiles upon the roofs.'

"The high pitched roofs and innumerable tiles on them everywhere met our eyes, and recalled the famous declaration.

"I should here tell you the

LUTHER'S HOUSE.

STORY OF SIEGFRIED AND THE NIBELUNG HEROES.

The early nations of Europe seem to have come out of the northwest of Asia. The Celts or Gauls came first; other tribes followed them. These latter tribes called themselves *Deutsch*, or *the people*. They settled between the Alps and the Baltic Sea. In time they came to be called Ger-men, or war-men. They lived in rude huts and held the lands in common. They were strong and brave and prosperous.

A TRIBE OF GERMANS ON AN EXPEDITION.

They worshipped the great god Woden. His day of worship was the fourth of the week; hence Woden's-day, or Wednesday.

Woden was an all-wise god. Ravens carried to him the news from earth. His temples were stone altars on desolate heaths, and human sacrifices were offered to him.

Woden had a celestial hall called Valhall, and thither he transported the souls of the brave; hence the name Valhalla.

There were supposed to be water gods in the rivers and elves throughout the forest. The heavens were peopled with minor gods, as well as the great gods, and the spirits of the unseen world could make themselves visible or invisible to men as they chose.

Most great nations have heroes of song sung by the poets, like those of Homer and Virgil. The early German hero was Siegfried, and the song or epic that celebrates his deeds is called the *Nibelungen Lied*. Its story is as follows.

In the Land of Mist there was a lovely river, where dwelt little people who could assume any form they wished. One of them was accustomed to change himself into an otter when he went to the river to fish. As he was fishing one day in this form he was caught by Loki, one of the great gods, who immediately despatched him and took off his skin.

When his brothers Fafner and Reginn saw what had been done, they reproved Loki severely, and demanded of him that he should fill the otter's skin with gold, and give it to them as an atonement for his great misdeed.

"I return the otter skin and give you the treasure you ask," said Loki; "but the gift shall bring you evil."

Their father took the treasure, and Fafner murdered his father to secure it to himself, and then turned into a dragon or serpent to guard it, and to keep his brother from finding it.

Reginn had a wonderful pupil, named Siegfried, a Samson among the inhabitants of the land. He was so strong that he could catch wild lions and hang them by the tail over the walls of the castle. Reginn persuaded this pupil to attack the serpent and to slay him.

Now Siegfried could understand the songs of birds; and the birds told him that Reginn intended to kill him; so he slew Reginn and himself possessed the treasure.

Serpents and dragons were called *worms* in Old Deutsch, and the Germans called the town where Siegfried lived Worms.

Siegfried had bathed himself in the dragon's blood, and the bath made his skin so hard that nothing could hurt him except in one spot. A leaf had fallen on this spot as he was bathing. It was between his shoulders.

Siegfried, like Samson, had a curious wife. His romances growing out of his love for this woman would fill a volume. She had learned where his one vulnerable spot lay. But she was a lovely lady, and the wedded pair lived very happily together at Worms.

At last a dispute arose between them and their relatives, and the latter sought to destroy Siegfried's life. His wife went for counsel to a supposed friend, but real enemy, named Hagen.

"Your husband is invulnerable," said Hagen.

"Yes, except in one spot."

FIFTH MEETING FOR RHINE STORIES.

"And you know the place?"

"Yes."

"Sew a patch on his garment over it, and I shall know how to protect him."

The poor wife had revealed a fatal secret. She sewed a patch on her husband's garment between the shoulders, and now thought him doubly secure.

THE MURDER OF SIEGFRIED.

There was to be a great hunting-match, and Siegfried entered into it as a champion. He rode forth in high spirits, but on his back was the fatal patch.

Hagen contrived that the wine should be left behind.

"That," he said, "will compel the hunters to lie down on their breasts to drink from the streams when they become thirsty. Then will come my opportunity."

He was right in his conjecture.

Siegfried became tired and thirsty. He rode up to a stream. He threw himself on his breast to drink, exposing his back, on which was the patch, revealing the vulnerable place.

There he was stabbed by a conspirator employed by Hagen.

They bore the dead body of the hero down the Rhine, and lamented the departed champion as the barque drifted on. The scene has been portrayed in art and song, and has left its impress on the poetic associations of the river. You will have occasion to recall this story again in connection with Drachenfels.

"Our fifth night on the Rhine was passed at Mayence, at the Hôtel de Hollande, near the landing-place of the Rhine steamers. The balconies and windows of the hotel afforded fine views of the river and of the Taunus Mountains.

"Mayence is said to have arisen by magic. The sorcerer Nequam wished for a new city; he came to this point of the Rhine, spoke the word, and the city rose. It is almost as old as the Christian era. Here the Twenty-second Roman legion came, after its return from the conquest of Jerusalem, and brought Christianity with it, through some of its early converts. It was one of the grand cities of Charlemagne, who erected a palace at Lower Ingelheim, and introduced the cultivation of the vine. Here lived Bishop Hatto, of bad repute, and good Bishop Williges.

"Here rose Gutenberg, the inventor of printing, and here Thorwaldsen's statue of the great inventor announces to the traveller what a great light of civilization appeared to the world.

"At Mayence we began the most delightful zigzag we had ever made, — a boat journey on the Rhine.

"'If you would see the Rhine of castles and vineyards,' said an English friend, 'hire a boat. The most famous river scenery in the world lies between Mayence and Cologne. If you take the railroad you will merely *escape* it in a few hours; if a steamboat, your curiosity will be excited, but not gratified; it will all vanish like a dream: take a boat, my good American friend, — take a boat.'

"Between Mayence and Bingen the Rhine attains its greatest breadth. It is studded with a hundred islands. Its banks are con-

MAYENCE.

tinuous vineyards. Here is the famous district called the Rheingau, which extends along the right bank of the river, where the Rhine wines are produced.

"It is all a luxurious wine-garden, — the Rheingau. The grapes purple beside ruins and convents, as well as on their low artificial trellises, and everywhere drink in the sunshine and grow luscious in the mellow air.

"Castles, palaces, ruins, towers, and quaint towns all mingle with the vineyards. A dreamy light hangs over the scene; the river is calm, and the boat drifts along in an atmosphere in which the spirit of romance seems to brood, as though indeed the world's fairy tales were true.

"We came in sight of Bingen.

"'We must stop there,' said Willie Clifton.

"'Why?' I asked curiously.

"'Because — well —

"For I was born at Bingen, — at Bingen on the Rhine."'

"He then repeated slowly and in a deep, tender voice the beginning of a poem that almost every schoolboy knows: —

'A soldier of the Legion lay dying in Algiers,
There was lack of woman's nursing, there was dearth of woman's tears;
But a comrade stood beside him, while his life-blood ebbed away,
And bent, with pitying glances, to hear what he might say.
The dying soldier faltered, as he took that comrade's hand,
And he said, "I nevermore shall see my own, my native land:
Take a message and a token to some distant friends of mine;
For I was born at Bingen, — at Bingen on the Rhine."'

"Bingen is a town of about seven thousand inhabitants, and is engaged in the wine trade. We visited the chapel of St. Rochus, on a hill near the town, because one of our party had somewhere read that Bulwer had said that the view from St. Rochus was the finest in the world.

"Again upon the river, all the banks seemed filled with castles, villages, and ruins. Every hill had its castle, every crag its gray tower. We drifted by the famous Mouse Tower, which stands at the end of an island meadow fringed with osier twigs. It is little better than a square tower of a common village church, nor is there any truth in the story that Southey's poem has associated with it. Poor Bishop Hatto, of evil name and memory! He died in 970, and the tower was not built until the thirteenth cen-

tury. For aught that is known, he was a good man; he certainly was not eaten up by rats or mice. The legend runs:—

"In the tenth century Hatto, Bishop of Fulda, was raised to the dignity of Archbishop of Mayence. He built a strong tower on the Rhine, wherein to collect tolls from the vessels that passed.

"A famine came to the Rhine countries. Hatto

had vast granaries, and the people came to him for bread. He refused them, and they importuned him. He bade them go into a large granary, one day, promising them relief. When they had entered the building, he barred the doors and set it on fire, and the famishing beggars, among whom were many women and children, were consumed.

"The bishop listened to the cries of the dying for mercy as the building was burning.

"'Hark!' he said, 'hear the rats squeak.'

"When the building fell millions of rats ran from the ruins to the bishop's palace. They filled all the rooms and attacked the people. The bishop was struck with terror.

'"I'll go to my tower on the Rhine," replied he;
"'T is the safest place in Germany:
The walls are high, and the shores are steep,
And the stream is strong, and the water deep."

'Bishop Hatto fearfully hastened away,
And he crossed the Rhine without delay,
And reached his tower, and barred with care
All windows, doors, and loopholes there.

'He laid him down and closed his eyes;
But soon a scream made him arise:
He started, and saw two eyes of flame
On his pillow, from whence the screaming came.

'He listened and looked; it was only the cat:
But the bishop he grew more fearful for that;
For she sat screaming, mad with fear
At the army of rats that were drawing near.

'For they have swam over the river so deep,
And they have climbed the shores so steep;
And up the tower their way is bent,
To do the work for which they were sent.

'They are not to be told by the dozen or score ;
By thousands they come, and by myriads and more :
Such numbers had never been heard of before,
Such a judgment had never been witnessed of yore.

'Down on his knees the bishop fell,
And faster and faster his beads did tell,
As, louder and louder drawing near,
The gnawing of their teeth he could hear.

'And in at the windows, and in at the door,
And through the walls, helter-skelter they pour,
And down from the ceiling, and up through the floor,
From the right and the left, from behind and before,
From within and without, from above and below,
And all at once to the bishop they go.

'They have whetted their teeth against the stones ;
And now they pick the bishop's bones :
They gnawed the flesh from every limb ;
For they were sent to do judgment on him !'

"We passed ruin after ruin which the boatman said were 'robber castles.'

"'And what do you mean by *robber* castles?' asked Herman.

"'The old lords of the Rhine used to collect tolls from the vessels that passed their estates. The tax was regarded as unjust, and hence the lords were themselves called robbers, and their castles robber castles.'

"One of these castles, called the *Pfalzgrafenstein*, is said to resemble a stone ship at anchor in the river. It was formerly a rock, with one little hut upon it, and it was associated with a touching incident of history.

"Louis le Debonnaire, the son of Charlemagne, became weary of state-craft and the crown. He felt that his end was near. He desired to die where he could hear the waves of the Rhine. He was taken to this rock, and there with the ebb of the river his troubled life ebbed away.

"Most of the old castles are built on the narrows of the river. These narrows are between high rocks and rocky hills. They are in the Middle Rhine, or between Mayence and Bonn. The Middle Rhine has some thirty conspicuous castles on its banks. It is sometimes

VIEW ON THE RHINE.

called the Castellated Rhine, and its narrows are termed the Castellated Rhine Pass.

"On, on we drifted. Every high rock seemed a gateway to some new scene of beauty; wonder followed wonder.

"And now the water seemed agitated. Dark rocks projected into the river; the view was intercepted.

"The boatman conversed in an animated way with me; and I looked up to a high rock with an interested expression and an incredulous smile.

"He turned to us quietly and said,—

"'This is the Lorelei Pass.'

"He presently added, —

"'That is the Lorelei.'

THE LORELEI

THE WONDERFUL STORY OF THE LORELEI.

Who has not heard it, repeated it in verse, echoed it in song? It is the best known of the Rhine tales, not because it is the most interesting, but because it is associated with the noblest scenery of the river, with poetry and music. It is hardly equal to such legends as the "Drachenfels" and the "Two Brothers," but it is lifted into historic prominence by its associations.

Still the story is richer in incident than the mere song would indicate. The origin and development of the popular legend is as follows: —

In the shadowy days of the Palatines of the Rhine, — shadowy because of ignorance and superstition, — the boatmen among the rocks above St. Goar on the Rhine used to fancy that they could see at night the form of a beautiful nymph on the "Lei," or high rock of the river. Her limbs were moulded of air; a veil of mist and gems covered her face; her hair was long and golden, and her eyes shone like the stars. Her robe was blue and glimmering like the waves, decked with water flowers and zoned with crystals. She was most distinctly seen by pale moonlight.

They called this recurring vision of mist and gems Lore, the enchantress. They believed that her favor brought good luck, but her ill will destruction.

Nothing could be more natural than for the simple fishermen to think that they saw a form of mist, very bright and lovely, above the rocks at night, when once the story had been told them.

In the days of superstition such a story was sure to grow.

It was said that this Undine of the Rhine, the enchantress Lore, had a most melodious and seductive voice. When she sang those who heard her listened spellbound. If the boatmen displeased her, she entranced them by her song, and drew them into the whirlpools under the rocks, where they disappeared forever. To the landsmen who offended her, she made the river appear like a road, and led them to fall over the rocks to destruction. With all her beauty and charms, she was the evil genius of the place.

Herman, the only son of the last Palatine, a youth of some fifteen summers, was delicate in health. Instead of devoting himself to chivalrous exercises, he gave his attention to music and song.

One night he and his father were descending the Rhine, when he felt an inspiration come over him to sing. His voice was silvery and flute-like, and breathed the emotional sentiment of the heart of youth. As the boat drew near the Lei, Lore, the enchantress, heard the song, and she herself became spellbound by the sentiment and deep feeling expressed in the mellifluent music.

She tried to answer him, but her voice failed.

As Herman grew to manhood his ill health disappeared, and his character changed. He became rugged and manly, and abandoned the arts for the chase, horsemanship, and the preparations for martial contests.

He became a renowned hunter. He rode the wildest steeds, and ventured into places and merrily blew his horn where no huntsman dared follow him.

The enchantress Lore, from the time she had heard his song, disappeared from the rocks. The change that came over his person and character seemed like enchantment: was the siren invisibly following him?

And now a strange thing began to startle him by its mystery. When alone, crossing a wild mountain or a ravine, he would seek to keep up a communication by shouting through his hands, —

"Hillo-ho-o-o-o!"

Immediately a sweet voice would answer, —

"Ho-o-o-o!"

He would follow the sound.

"Hillo-ho-o-o-o!"

"Ho-o-o-o!"

It always led him towards the Lei.

He became alarmed at this occurrence. He believed that he was followed by a spirit, and that a spell was upon him, which boded destruction. He resolved to abandon the chase and devote himself to the arts again.

He was sitting by the window of the castle on a summer evening. A purple mist lay on the forests and river, and the moon poured her light over it, making all things appear like an enchanted realm.

He heard a nightingale singing in the woods. Did ever a bird sing like that? He listened. There was a witchery in the song. He rose and went into the woods. The song filled the air like a shower of golden notes. He followed it. It retreated. He went on. But the song, more and more enchanting and alluring, floated into the shadowy distance. He found himself at last on the Lei.

He beheld there a dazzling grotto, full of stalactites, and a nymph of wondrous beauty on a coral throne. He felt his being thrill with love. He was about to enter the grotto, when, oh thought of darkness and horror! the recollection of the enchantress came to him, and he crossed his bosom and broke the spell. He hurried home with a beating heart.

But the temptation and vision had proved fatal to him. He was never himself again. He dreamed constantly of Lore. All his longings were for her.

At eve he would hear the same nightingale singing. He would long to follow the voice. It inflamed his love. His will, his senses, all that made life desirable, were yielding to the fatal passion.

He went to a good priest for advice.

"Father Walter, what shall I do?"

"Shake off the spell, or it will end in your ruin."

One day Herman and the priest went fishing on the Rhine. The boat drifted near the Lei. The moon rose in full splendor in the clear sky, strewing the water with countless gems.

Herman took a lute and filled the air with music. It was answered from the Lei. Oh, how wonderful! The air seemed entranced with the spiritual melody. Herman was beside himself with delight. The priest also heard it.

"The Lore! In the name of the Virgin, let us make for the shore!"

Herman's eyes were fixed on the rock. There she sat, the siren!

The priest plied the oar, to turn the boat back.

But nearer, nearer drifted the boat to the rock.

Nearer and nearer!

The moon poured her white light upon the crags.

Nearer and nearer!

There was a shock.

The boat was shivered like glass.
Walter crossed himself, and floated on the waves to the shore.
But Herman — he was never seen again!

Mr. Beal's narrative nearly filled the evening. A few stories were told by other members of the Club, but they were chiefly from Grimm, and hence are somewhat familiar. Charlie Leland closed the meeting with a free translation of a poem from Kerner.

Justinus Kerner was born in Ludwigsburg, in 1786. He was a physician and a poet. He belonged to the spiritualistic school of poets, and his illustrations of the power of mind over matter, in both prose and poetry, are often very forcible. The following poem will give you a view of his estimate of physical as compared with mental power: —

IN THE OLD CATHEDRAL.

In the vaults of the dim cathedral,
 In the gloaming, weird and cold,
Are the coffins of old King Ottmar,
 And a poet, renowned of old.

The king once sat in power,
 Enthroned in pomp and pride,
And his crown still rests upon him,
 And his falchion rusts beside.

And near to the king the poet
 Has slumbered in darkness long,
But he holds in his hands, as an emblem,
 The harp of immortal song.

Hark! 'tis the castles falling!
 Hark! 'tis the war-cry dread!
But the monarch's sword is not lifted,
 There, in the vaults of the dead!

List to the vernal breezes!
 List to the minstrels' strain!
'T is the poet's song they are singing,
 And the poet lives again.

CHAPTER X.

NIGHT THE SIXTH.

THE BEAUTIFUL RHINE. — COBLENTZ. — A ZIGZAG TO WEIMAR. — GOETHE AND SCHILLER. — THE STRANGE STORY OF FAUST. — FAUST IN ART. — THE SEVEN MOUNTAINS. — THE DRACHENFELS. — THE STORY OF THE DRAGON. — STORIES OF FREDERICK THE GREAT. — THE UNNERVED HUSSAR.

R. BEAL occupied much of the time this evening. He thus continued the narrative of travel: —

"From St. Goar to Boppard, two stations at which the Rhine boats call, is about an hour's run; but the journey is an unfailing memory. The rocky walls of the river, the continuous villages, the quaint churches amid the vineyards and cherry orchards, the mossy meadows about the mountains, the white-kerchiefed villagers, present so many varied and delightful objects, that the eye feasts on beauty, and wonders expectantly at what the next turn of the river will reveal. The rock shadows in the water contrast with the bright scenes above the river, and add an impression of grandeur to the effect of the whole, like shadows on the cathedral walls that heighten the effect of the rose-colored windows. Beautiful, beautiful, is the Rhine.

"Grand castles, perched on high cliffs and mountain walls, surprise us, delight us, and vanish behind us, as the boat moves on; — the Brother Castles, Marksburg, the mountain palace Solzenfels, with their lofty, gloomy, and barbaric grandeur, reminding one always of times whose loss the mind does not regret.

"And now a beautiful city comes in view, nestled at the foot of the hills, and protected by a stupendous fortress on the opposite side of the river. The fortress is Ehrenbreitstein, the Gibraltar of the Rhine, capable of holding an army of men. It is a great arsenal now, well garrisoned in peace as in war; in short, it may be called the watch on the Rhine.

EHRENBREITSTEIN.

"The lovely city under its guns, on the opposite side of the river, is Coblentz. It is a gusset of houses, a V-shaped city, at the confluence of the Rhine and Moselle. The Romans called it the city of the Confluence, or Confluentia; hence, corrupted, it is known as Coblentz.

"It is the half-way city between Cologne and Mayence, and a favor-

GOETHE'S PROMENADE.

ite resting place of tourists. The summer residence of the King of Germany is here.

"From Coblentz we made a détour into the heart of Germany, going by rail to Weimar, once called the Athens of the North. It was once the literary centre of Germany. Here lived Goethe, Schiller, Wieland, and Herder. What the English Lake District, in the days of Wordsworth, Southey, Coleridge, Christopher North, and De Quincey was once to England, what Cambridge and Concord have been to America in the best days of its authors and poets, Weimar was to Germany at the beginning of the present century. We went there to visit the tombs and statues of Goethe, and to gain a better knowledge of the works of these poets from the associations of their composition.

"Weimar is a quaint provincial-looking town on the river Ilm. It has some sixteen thousand inhabitants, and is the residence of the Grand Duke of Saxe-Weimar. The grounds of the palace are wonderfully beautiful. They extend along the river, and communicate with a summer palace called Belvedere.

"We visited the tombs of the two great poets. They are found beneath a small chapel in the Grand Ducal burial vault. The Grand Duke Charles Augustus desired that the bodies of the two poets should be interred one on each side of him; but this was forbidden by the usages of the court.

"In the old Stadtkirche, built in 1400, are the tombs of the ancient dukes, now forgotten. Among them is that of Duke Bernard, who died in 1639. He was the friend of Gustavus Adolphus, and one of the most powerful of the leaders of the Reformation.

"Goethe, the most gifted of the German poets, and the most accomplished man of his age, was born at Frankfort-on-the-Main, in 1749. In 1775 he made the intimate acquaintance of Charles Augustus, Grand Duke of Saxe-Weimar, who induced him to take up his residence at Weimar, the capital. Here he held many public offices, and at last became minister of state. He died at the age of eighty-four.

"Goethe's most popular work is a novel called *The Sorrows of Werther*, but his great and enduring work is *Faust*, a dramatic poem, in which his great genius struggles with the problems of good and evil.

"His life was full of beautiful friendships. In 1787 Schiller, the second in rank of great German poets, was invited to reside at Weimar. Goethe became most warmly attached to him, and the two pursued their high literary callings together. The literary circle now consisted of Goethe, Schiller, Wieland, Herder, and the Grand Duke. It was the golden age of German literature.

THE STRANGE STORY OF FAUST.

No myth of the Middle Ages has had so large a growth and so long a life as this.

It has been made the subject of books, pamphlets, and articles almost without number. The Faust literature in Germany would fill a library.

In painting, especially of the Holland school, the dark subject as prominently appears. It is also embodied in sculpture.

But it is in poetry and music that it found a place that carried it over the world. It was made the subject of Marlowe's drama, of Goethe's greatest poem, and it is sung in three of the greatest operas of modern times.

But to the legend.

About the year 1490 there was born at Roda, in the Duchy of Saxe-Weimar, a child whose fame was destined to fill the world of superstition, fable, and song. He was named John Faustus, or Faust.

He studied medicine, became an alchemist, and was possessed with a consuming desire to learn the secrets of life and of the spiritual world.

He studied magic, and his thirst for knowledge of the occult sciences grew. He wished to know how to prolong life, to change base metals to gold, to do things at once by the power of the will.

One night, as he was studying, the Evil One appeared before him.

"I will reveal to you all the secrets you are seeking, and will enable you to do anything you wish by the power of the will alone — "

Dr. Faustus was filled with an almost insane delight.

" — On one condition."

"Name it."

"That I shall have your soul in return."
"When?"
"At the end of twenty-four years — at this time of night — midnight."
"I shall have pleasure?"

FAUST SIGNING.

"Pleasure."
"Gold?"
"Gold."
"I shall know the secrets of nature?"
"The secrets of nature."
"I may do what I like at will?"
"At will."

"I will sign the compact."

"Sign!"

Faust signed his name to a compact that was to give the Evil One his soul for twenty-four years of pleasure, gold, and knowledge, that were to come to an end at midnight.

"I will give you an attendant," said the Evil One, "to help you."

He caused a dark but very elegant gentleman to appear, whom he presented to Faust as Mephistopheles.

Dr. Faustus and Mephistopheles now began to travel into all lands, performing wonders to the amazement of all people wherever they went.

In a wine-cellar at Leipsig, where he and Mephistopheles were drinking, some gay fellows said, —

"Faust, make grapes grow on a vine on this table."

"Be silent."

There was dead silence.

A vine began to grow from the table, and presently it bore a bunch of grapes for each of the revellers.

FAUST AND MEPHISTOPHELES.

"Take your knives and cut a cluster for each."

There was an explosion. Faust and Mephistopheles were seen flying out of the window; the *window* is still shown in Leipsig. The vine had disappeared, and each of the revellers found himself with his knife over his nose, about to cut it off, supposing it to be a cluster of grapes.

The wonders that it is claimed that Dr. Faustus did in the twenty-four years fill volumes. The Faust marvels have gathered to themselves the fables of centuries.

The twenty-four years came to an end at last. Faust became gloomy, and retired to Rimlich, at the inn, among his old friends.

The fatal night came.

"Should you hear noises in my chamber to-night, do not disturb me," he said, on parting from his companions to go to his room.

Near midnight a tempest arose, — a wild, strange tempest. The winds were like demons. It thundered and the air was full of tongues of lightning.

At midnight there was heard a fearful shriek in Faust's chamber.

The next morning the room was found bespattered with blood, and the body of Faust was missing. The broken remains of the alchemist were discovered at last in a back yard on a heap of earth.

This was the village story. It grew as such a dark myth would grow in the superstitious times in which it started. Goethe created the character of Marguerite and added it to the fable. The transformation of Faust from extreme old age to youth was also added. The opera makers have greatly enlarged even the narrative of Goethe; in the latest evolution, Mephistopheles is summoned into the courts of heaven and sent forth to tempt Faust, and Faust is shown visions of the Greek vale of Tempe and Helen of Troy.

Faust has come to be a synonym of the great problem of Good and Evil; the contest between virtue and vice, temptation and ruin, temptation and moral triumph. It is not a good story in any of its evolutions, but it is one that to know is almost essential to intelligence.

"Returning to Coblentz, we passed our sixth night on the Rhine. We there hired a boatman to take us to Bonn. Between Coblentz and Andernach we passed what are termed the Rhine Plains. These are some ten miles long, and are semicircled by volcanic mountains, whose fires have long been dead.

"We now approached the Seven Mountains, among which is the Drachenfels, famous in fable and song. These are called: Lohrberg,

1,355 feet; Neiderstromberg, 1,066 feet; Oelberg, 1,429 feet; Wolkenberg, 1,001 feet; Drachenfels, 1,056 feet; Petenberg, 1,030 feet; Lowenberg, 1,414 feet.

"The Drachenfels is made picturesque by an ancient ruin, and it is these ancient ruins, and associations of old history, that make the Rhine the most interesting river in the world. Apart from its castles and traditions, it is not more beautiful than the Hudson, the Upper Ohio, or the Mississippi between St. Paul and Winona. But the Rhine displays the ruined arts of two thousand years.

"The Drachenfels has its wonderful story. It is said that Siegfried killed the Dragon there. The so-called Dragon Cave or Rock is there, and of this particular dragon many curious tales are told.

"In the early days of Christianity the cross was regarded as something more than a mere emblem of faith. It was believed to possess miracle-working power.

"In a rocky cavern of the Drachenfels, in ancient times, there lived a Dragon of most hideous form. He had a hundred teeth, and his head was so large that he could swallow several victims at a time. His body was of enormous length, and in form like an alligator's, and he had a tail like a serpent.

"The pagans of the Rhine worshipped this monster and offered to him human sacrifices.

"In one of the old wars between rival princes, a Christian girl was taken captive, and the pagan priest commanded that she should be made an offering to the Dragon.

"It was the custom of the pagans to bind their sacrifices to the Dragon alive to a tree near his cave at night. At sunrise he would come out and devour them.

"They led the lovely Christian maiden to a spot near the cave, and bound her to a tree.

"It was starlight. Priests and warriors with torches had conducted the maiden to the fatal spot, and stood at a little distance from the victim, waiting for the sunrise.

A CLEFT IN THE MOUNTAINS

"The priests chanted their wild hymns, and the light at last began to break and to crown the mountains and be scattered over the blue river.

"The roar of the monster was heard. The rocks trembled, and he appeared. He approached the maiden, bound to an oak.

"Her eyes were raised in prayer towards heaven.

"As the Dragon approached the victim, she drew from her bosom a crucifix, and held it up before him.

"As soon as he saw it, he began to tremble. He fell to the earth as if smitten. He lost all power and rolled down the rocks, a shapeless mass, into the Rhine.

"The pagans released the girl.

"'By what power have you done this?' they asked.

"'By this,' said the maiden, stretching out the cross in her hand. 'I am a Christian.'

"'Then we will become Christians,' said the pagans, and they led the lovely apostle away to be their teacher. Her first convert was one of the rival princes, whom she married. Their descendants were among the most eminent of the early Christian families of the Seven Mountains of the Rhine.

"Such is the fable as told by the monks of old. The figure of the power of the cross over the serpent, employed in early Christian writings, undoubtedly was its origin, but how it became associated with the story of the captive maiden it would be hard to tell."

Master Lewis introduced the story-telling of the evening by anecdote pictures of

FREDERICK THE GREAT.

Frederick the Great, King of Prussia, was born in 1712. He was a wilful youth, and his father subjected him to such severe discipline that he revolted against it, and, like other boys not of royal blood, formed a plan of running away from home. His father discovered the plot, and caused his son's most intimate friend, who had assisted him in it, to be put to death, and made the execution as terrible as possible. He early came to hate his father, his father's religion, and everything that the old king most liked. His father was indeed a hard, stern man, of colorless character; but he managed the affairs of state so prudently that he left his undutiful son a powerful army and a full treasury, and to these as much as to any noble qualities of mind or soul the latter owed the resources by which he gained the title THE GREAT.

His mother was a daughter of George I. Frederick loved her, and from her he inherited a taste for music and literature, like many of the family of the Georges. He formed an intimate friendship with Voltaire, the French infidel writer, and interested himself in the French infidelity of the period, which was a reaction against the corrupt and degenerate French church.

He entered the field as a soldier in 1741, and was victorious again and again in the two Silesian wars. The Seven Years' War, begun in 1756, gained for him a position of great influence among the rulers of Europe. He was prudent, like his father; his government was wise, well ordered, and liberal, and he left to his successor a full treasury, a great and famous army, enlarged territory, and the prestige of a great name.

The family affairs of kings during the last century were in rather a queer state, as the following story of Frederick's marriage will show.

The prince was told that his father was studying the characters of the young ladies of the courts of Europe in order to select a suitable wife for him. He admired talent, brilliancy, wit, and he said in substance to the Minister of State, —

"Influence my father if you can to obtain for me a gifted and elegant princess. Of all things in the world I would hate to have a dull and commonplace wife."

His father made choice of the Princess Elizabeth Christine of Brunswick, a girl famous for her awkwardness and stupidity.

The prince did everything in his power to prevent the marriage. But the old king declared that he should marry her, and the wedding ceremony was arranged, Frederick in the mean time protesting that he held the bride in utter detestation.

Frederick had a sister whom he dearly loved, Wilhelmina. Two days after his marriage, he introduced the bride to her, and said, —

"This is a sister whom I adore. She has had the goodness to promise that *she* will take care of you and give you good advice. I wish you to do nothing without her consent. Do you understand?"

VOLTAIRE.

The young bride, scarcely eighteen, was speechless. She expected "care" and "advice" from her husband, and not from his sister.

Wilhelmina embraced her tenderly.

Frederick waited for an answer to his question. But she stood dumb.

"Plague take the *blockhead!*" he at last exclaimed, and with this compliment began the long and sorrowful story of her wedded life.

She was a good woman and bore her husband's neglect with patience. Strangely enough, in his old age Frederick came to love her; for he discovered, after a prejudice of years, that she had a noble souL

Frederick died in 1786. In his will he made a most liberal allowance for his wife, and bore testimony to her excellent character, saying that she never had caused him the least discontent, and her incorruptible virtue was worthy of love and consideration.

She survived the king eleven years.

Willie Clifton related a true story.

THE UNNERVED HUSSAR.

A man once entered the vaults of a church by night, to rob a corpse of a valuable ring. In replacing the lid he nailed the tail of his coat to the coffin, and when he started up to leave, the coffin clung to him and moved towards him.

Supposing the movement to be the work of invisible hands, his nervous system received such a shock that he fell in a fit, and was found where he fell, by the sexton, on the following morning.

Now, had the fellow been honestly engaged, it is not likely that the blunder would have happened; and even had it occurred, he doubtless would have discovered at once the cause.

But very worthy people are sometimes affected by superstitious fear, and run counter to the dictates of good sense and sound judgment.

A magnificent banquet was once given by a lord, in a very ancient castle, on the confines of Germany. Among the guests was an officer of hussars, distinguished for great self-possession and bravery.

Many of the guests were to remain in the castle during the night; and the gallant hussar was informed that one of them must occupy a room reputed to be haunted, and was asked if he had any objections to accepting the room for himself.

He declared that he had none whatever, and thanked his host for the honor conferred upon him by the offer. He, however, expressed a wish that no trick might be played upon him, saying that such an act might be followed by very serious consequences, as he should use his pistols against whatever disturbed the peace of the room.

He retired after midnight, leaving his lamp burning; and, wearied by the festivities, soon fell asleep. He was presently awakened by the sound of music, and, looking about the apartment, saw at the opposite end, three phantom ladies, grotesquely attired, singing a mournful dirge.

The music was artistic, rich, and soothing, and the hussar listened for a time,

THE UNNERVED HUSSAR.

highly entertained. The piece was one of unvarying sadness, and, however seductive at first, after a time lost its charm.

The officer, addressing the musical damsels, remarked that the music had become rather monotonous, and asked them to change the tune. The singing continued in the same mournful cadences. He became impatient, and exclaimed, —

"Ladies, this is an impertinent trick, for the purpose of frightening me. I shall take rough means to stop it, if it gives me any further trouble."

He seized his pistols in a manner that indicated his purpose. But the mysterious ladies remained, and the requiem went on.

"Ladies," said the officer, "I will wait five minutes, and then shall fire, unless you leave the room."

The figures remained, and the music continued. At the expiration of the time, the officer counted twenty in a loud, measured voice, and then, taking deliberate aim, discharged both of his pistols.

The ladies were unharmed, and the music was uninterrupted. The unexpected result of his violence threw him into a state of high nervous excitement, and, although his courage had withstood the shock of battle, it now yielded to his superstitious fears. His strength was prostrated, and a severe illness of some weeks' continuance followed.

Had the hussar held stoutly to his own sensible philosophy, that he had no occasion to fear the spirits of the invisible world, nothing serious would have ensued. The damsels sung in another apartment, and their figures were made to appear in the room occupied by the hussar, by the effect of a mirror. The whole was a trick, carefully planned, to test the effect of superstitious fear on one of the bravest of men.

In no case should a person be alarmed at what he suspects to be supernatural. A cool investigation will show, in most cases, that the supposed phenomenon may be easily explained. It might prove a serious thing for one to be frightened by a nightcap on a bedpost, for a fright affects unfavorably the nervous system, but a nightcap on a bedpost is in itself a very harmless thing.

The sixth evening closed with an original poem by Mr. Beal.

CHAPTER XI.

COLOGNE.

BONN. — HOLY COLOGNE. — THE STORY OF THE MYSTERIOUS ARCHITECT. — "UNFINISHED AND UNKNOWN." — VISIT TO COLOGNE CATHEDRAL. — THE TOMB OF THE MAGI. — THE CHURCH OF SKULLS. — QUEER RELICS. — THE STORY AND LEGEND OF CHARLEMAGNE. — THE STORY AND LEGEND OF BARBAROSSA.

E emerged from the majestic circle of the Seven Mountains, the most beautiful part of the Rhine scenery, and broad plains again met our view. The river ran smoothly, the Middle Rhine was passed, Bonn was in view, and there we dismissed our boatman.

"We stopped in Bonn only a short time. We went to the Market-place and walked past the University, which was once a palace.

"We took the train at Bonn for Cologne, in order to pass rapidly over a part of the Rhine scenery said to be comparatively uninteresting.

" Holy Cologne !

" The Rome of the Northern Empire! The ecclesiastical capital of the ancient German church !

" The unfinished cathedral towers over the city like a mountain. 'Unfinished?' Everything has a legend here, and a marvellous one, and the unfinished cathedral stands like a witness to such a tale.

" Above Cologne the river runs broad, a blue-green mirror amid dumpy willows and lanky poplars, and the windmills on its banks throw their arms about like giants at play. The steamers swarm in

CATHEDRAL OF COLOGNE.

the bright waters; at evening their lights are like will-o'-the-wisps. The long bridge of boats opens; a steamer passes, followed by a crowd of boats; it closes, and the waiting crowd upon it hurry over. The Rhine at night here presents a most animated scene.

"The river seems alive, but the city looks dead. There is a faded glory on everything. There are steeples and steeples, towers and towers. Cologne is said to have had at one time as many churches as there are days in the year. But life has gone out of them; they are like deserted houses. They belonged to the religious period of evolution, and are like geologic formations now, — history that has had its day, and left its tombstone.

"Cologne is as old as Rome in her glory, — older than the Christian era. She was the second great city of the Church in the Middle Ages.

"Cologne is full of wonders in stone and marble, wonders in legend and story as well; and among these the cathedral holds the first place, in both art and fable.

THE MYSTERIOUS ARCHITECT.

In the thirteenth century — so the story goes — Archbishop Conrad determined to erect a cathedral that should surpass any Christian temple in the world.

Who should be the architect?

He must be a man of great genius, and his name would become immortal.

There *was* a wonderful builder in Cologne, and the Archbishop went to him with his purpose, and asked him to attempt the design.

"It must not only surpass anything in the past, but anything that may arise in the future."

The architect was awed in view of such a stupendous undertaking.

"It will carry my name down the ages," he thought; "I will sacrifice everything to success."

He dreamed; he fasted and prayed.

He made sketch after sketch and plan after plan, but they all proved unworthy of a temple that should be one of the grandest monuments of the piety of the time, and one of the glories of future ages.

In his dreams an exquisite image of a temple rose dimly before him. When he awoke, he could vaguely recall it, but could not reproduce it. The ideal haunted him and yet eluded him.

He became disheartened. He wandered in the fields, absorbed in thought. The beautiful apparition of the temple would suddenly fill him with delight; then it would vanish, as if it were a mockery.

One day he was wandering along the Rhine, absorbed in thought.

"Oh," he said, "that the phantom temple would appear to me, and linger but for a moment, that I could grasp the design."

He sat down on the shore, and began to draw a plan with a stick on the sand.

"That is it," he cried with joy.

"Yes, that is it, indeed," said a mocking voice behind him.

He looked around, and beheld an old man.

"That is it," the stranger hissed; "that is the Cathedral of Strasburg."

He was shocked. He effaced the design on the sand.

He began again.

"There it is," he again exclaimed with delight.

"Yes," chuckled the old man. "That is the Cathedral of Amiens."

The architect effaced the picture on the sand, and produced another.

"Metz," said the old man.

He made yet another effort.

"Antwerp!"

"O my master," said the despairing architect, "you mock me. Produce a design for me yourself."

"On one condition."

"Name it."

"You shall give me yourself, soul and body!"

The affrighted architect began to say his prayers, and the old man suddenly disappeared.

The next day he wandered into a forest of the Seven Mountains, still thinking of his plan. He chanced to look up the mountain side, when he beheld the queer old man again; he was now leaning on a staff on a rocky wall.

He lifted his staff and began to draw a picture on a rock behind him. The lines were of fire.

Oh, how beautiful, how grand, how glorious, it all was!

THE MYSTERIOUS ARCHITECT.

Fretwork, spandrels, and steeples. It *was* — it *was* the very design that had haunted the poor architect, that flitted across his mind in dreams but left no memory.

"Will you have my plan?" asked the old man.

"I will do all you ask."

"Meet me at the city gate to-morrow at midnight."

The architect returned to Cologne, the image of the marvellous temple glowing in his mind.

"I shall be immortal," he said; "my name will never die. But," he added, "it is the price of my soul. No masses can help me, doomed, doomed forever!"

He told his strange story to his old nurse on his return home.

She went to consult the priest.

"Tell him," said the priest to the old woman, "to secure the design before he signs the contract. As soon as he gets the plan into his hand let him present to the old man, who is a demon, the relics of the martyrs and the sign of the cross."

At midnight he appeared at the gate. There stood the little old man.

"Here is your design," said the latter, handing him a roll of parchment. "Now you shall sign the bond that gives me yourself in payment."

The architect grasped the plan.

"Satan, begone!" he thundered; "in the name of this cross, and of St. Ursula, begone!"

"Thou hast foiled me," said the old man, his eyes glowing in the darkness like fire. "But I will have my revenge. Your church may in time be completed, but your name shall never be known in the future to mankind."

"The Cathedral of Cologne is at last finished, but its architect's name is unknown. It may harm the story, but it is but just to say that many of the old cathedrals of Europe are in these respects like that of Cologne.

"We were impatient to visit the cathedral on our arrival at Cologne. The structure stood as it were *over* the city, like its presiding genius; and so it was. Wherever we went the great roofs loomed above us in the air.

"The interior did not disappoint us, even after all we had seen in other cathedral towns. It was like a forest: the columns were like tree stems of a vast open woodland, the groined arches appearing like interweaving boughs. The gorgeous windows were like a sunset through the trees. The air was dusky in the arches, but near the lofty windows vivid with color.

"It was Sunday. The service had begun. It was like a pageant, an opera. The organ was pouring a solemn chant through the far arches, like fall winds among the trees. There was a flute-like gush of music, far off and mysterious, like birds. It came from the boy-choristers. Priests in glittering garments were kneeling before the cupola-crowned altar; there rose a cloud of incense from silver censers, and the organ thundered again, like the storm gathering over the woods. At the side of the altar stood the archiepiscopal throne, half in shadow amid the tall lights, red and gold; amid the piles of barbaric splendor, canopies, carvings, emblems.

"We visited the chapels on the following day. In one of them a Latin inscription tells the visitor, —

"'HERE REPOSE THE THREE BODIES OF THE HOLY MAGI.'

"The guide said, —

"'This is the tomb of the Three Kings of Cologne.'

"'The Wise Men of the East who came to worship at the cradle at Bethlehem.'

"'Ask him how he *got* them,' said Willie.

"'The Empress Helena, mother of Constantine, recovered them and sent them to Milan. When Frederick Barbarossa took the city of Milan, he received them among the spoils and sent them to Cologne. The names of the Magi were Gaspar, Melchior, Balthazar.'

"'Do you believe the legend?' asked Willie.

"'I do not know; we shall find things harder than this to believe, I fancy, as we go on.'

"And we did.

"Leaving the tomb, — a pile of jewels, — we went out, and near the

ST. MARTIN'S CHURCH, COLOGNE.

outskirts of the city found the famous Church of Skulls,—a gilded ossuary, associated with a mediæval legend. It was full of cabinets of bones, said to be those of eleven thousand virgins slain for their faith by the Huns.

"Here we were shown—

"*A part of the rod with which the Saviour was scourged.*

"*A thorn from the crown of thorns,— the Spicula.*

"*The pitcher in which Jesus turned water into wine.*

"'The Mediæval Church,' said our English-speaking guide, who had little faith in the genuineness of the relics, 'has exhibited some relics from time to time that would repay a long and arduous pilgrimage if they were what they purported to be; as, for instance, a feather of the angel Gabriel, the snout of a seraph, a ray from the star of Bethlehem, *two* skulls of the same saint,—one taken when the departed saint was somewhat younger, as flippantly explained to an astonished tourist, who found in two cities the same consecrated cranium.

"'But of all the relics of which we ever read, some Germans who visited Italy in search of these precious mementos received the most remarkable.

"'One of these gentlemen, having applied to an ecclesiastic for some memento of Scripture history which he could take back to Germany, was both astonished and delighted by receiving a carefully prepared package, which he was assured contained a veritable leg of the ass on which was made the triumphal entry into Jerusalem, when the people strewed palm branches in the way and shouted hosannas.

"'He was enjoined to keep the treasure a secret until he reached home, which injunction he scrupulously obeyed.

"'Arriving in Germany, he disclosed to his four companions the wonderful relic. They were much surprised, for each had been secretly intrusted with the same remarkable treasure. So it appeared that the ass had *five* legs, which, of itself, would have been something of a miracle.

"'Whether these wiseacres ever visited the Latin kingdom in search of relics again I am not apprised.'

"Cologne is full of relics. The people regard them with reverence; they serve the purpose of scriptural object-teaching to them. But they only shock the tourist who has been educated to believe that religion is a spiritual life, and that Christ's kingdom is a spiritual kingdom, and not of this world."

Several of the stories related by the boys this evening were historical.

THE STORY AND LEGEND OF CHARLEMAGNE.

Charles the Great, or Charlemagne, King of the Franks and Roman Emperor, was born, probably at Aix-la-Chapelle, in 742. His empire at first embraced the larger part of what is now France and Germany, but it extended under his wars until at last it nearly filled Europe, and he wore the crown of Rome and the West. Napoleon, at the height of his power, governed nearly the whole territory that was once ruled by the mighty Charlemagne.

He was one of the greatest and wisest men in the history of the world. He encouraged learning, and opened a school in his palace; he maintained morality and aimed to spread Christianity throughout the world.

The Saxons were heathens. They honored a great idol called the Irmansaul. They were opposed to Charlemagne, and constantly threatened his frontiers.

Charlemagne invaded their country, overthrew the great image, and after many struggles reduced the people to submission. In accordance with the rude customs of the time, he compelled them to accept Christianity and receive baptism. He is said to have baptized the prisoners of war with his own hand. He divided Saxony into eight bishoprics, and supported the bishops with guards of soldiers. We should look upon such missionary work as this as very questionable to-day, although enlightened nations of this age have sometimes adopted a policy in dealing with other countries that is as open to criticism and censure.

The Pope of Rome became involved in troubles with the Lombards. He appealed for help to the victorious King of the Franks, the recognized champion of the Church. Charlemagne crossed the Alps, conquered Lombardy, and crowned himself with the iron crown of the ancient Lombard kings.

CHARLEMAGNE IN THE SCHOOL OF THE PALACE

He then repaired to Rome and entered the city in triumph. As he came to St. Peter's he stooped to kiss the steps in memory of the illustrious men that had trodden it before him. The Pope there received him in great ceremony, and the choir chanted, "Blessed is he that cometh in the name of the Lord."

He now became the most powerful monarch in the world. He gained great victories over the Moors in Spain, and it was in one of the mountain passes there that the chivalrous young Roland, of heroic song, perished. His lands stretched from the Baltic Sea to the Mediterranean.

In the year 800 he went to Rome. It was Christmas Day. He entered the basilica of St. Peter's to attend Mass. He approached the altar, and bowed to pray. The Pope secretly uplifted the crown of the world and placed it upon his head.

The people shouted, "*Long live Charles Augustus, crowned of God, Emperor of the Romans!*"

From this time Charlemagne was the Kaiser, or Cæsar, of the Holy Roman Empire on the Tiber and the Rhine.

The Rhine was loved by Charlemagne. He lived much on its borders, and he was buried near it, in a church that he had founded, at Aix-la-Chapelle.

> "I 'd dwell where Charlemagne looked down,
>   And, turning to his peers,
> Exclaimed: 'Behold, for this fair land
>   I 've prayed and fought for years.'
> Then all the Rhine towers shook to hear
>   The earthquake of their cheers.
>
> "That day the tide ran crimson red
>   (But not with Rhenish wine);
> Not with those vintage streams that through
>   The green leaves gush and shine:
> 'T was blood that from the Lombard ranks
>   Rushed down into the Rhine.
>
> "'T was here the German soldiers flocked,
>   Burning with love and pride,
> And threw their muskets down to kiss
>   The soil with French blood dyed.
> 'The Rhine, dear Rhine!' ten thousand men,
>   Kneeling together, cried."
>
> THORNBURY.

There is a beautiful legend that Charlemagne visits the Rhine yearly and blesses the vintage. He comes in a golden robe, and crosses the river on a golden bridge, and the bells of heaven chime above him as he fulfils his peaceful mission. The fine superstition is celebrated in music and verse.

> "By the Rhine, the emerald river,
> How softly glows the night!
> The vine-clad hills are lying
> In the moonbeams' golden light.
>
> "And on the hillside walketh
> A kingly shadow down,
> With sword and purple mantle,
> And heavy golden crown.
>
> "'T is Charlemagne, the emperor,
> Who, with a powerful hand,
> For many a hundred years
> Hath ruled in German land.
>
> "From out his grave in Aachen
> He hath arisen there,
> To bless once more his vineyards,
> And breathe their fragrant air.
>
> "By Rudesheim, on the water,
> The moon doth brightly shine,
> And buildeth a bridge of gold
> Across the emerald Rhine.
>
> "The emperor walketh over,
> And all along the tide
> Bestows his benediction
> On the vineyards far and wide.
>
> "Then turns he back to Aachen
> In his grave-sleep to remain,
> Till the New Year's fragrant clusters
> Shall call him forth again."
>   EMANUEL GEIBEL.

THE STORY AND LEGEND OF BARBAROSSA.

Frederick of Germany was a very handsome man. There was a tinge of red in his beard, and for that reason he came to be called Frederick Barbarossa. He was an ambitious man, and he went to Rome to be crowned.

CHARLEMAGNE INFLICTING BAPTISM UPON THE SAXONS

It was a time of rival popes, and Barbarossa entered into the long controversy, which would make a history of itself. He captured Milan, and levelled the city. The sacred relics in the churches were sent to enrich the churches of Germany. Among these were the reputed bodies of the three Wise Men of the East; these were sent to Cologne, and are still exhibited there amid heaps of jewels.

Barbarossa was constantly at war with popes and kings: he gained victories

THE GERMANS ON AN EXPEDITION.

and suffered reverses; but his career was theatrical and popular in those rude times, and he was regarded as a very good monarch as kings went.

He once held a great peace festival at Mentz, to which came forty thousand knights. A camp of tents of silk and gold was set up by the Rhine, and musicians, called minnesingers, delighted the nobles and ladies with songs of heroes and knights. The songs and ballads then sung became famous, and this festival may be said to be the beginning of musical art in music-loving Germany.

Europe was now startled with the news that the Saracens under Saladin had taken Jerusalem. Barbarossa was about inaugurating a new war with the Pope; but when this news came he and the Pope became reconciled, and he resolved to go on a crusade.

He was an old man now, but he entered into the crusade with the fiery spirit of youth. His war-cry was,—

"Christ reigns! Christ conquers!"

He won a great victory at Iconium.

There was a swift, cold river near the battle-field, called Kaly Kadmus. A few days after the victory, Barbarossa went into it to bathe. He was struck by a chill and sank into the rapid current, and was drowned. He was seventy years of age. His body was found and interred at Antioch.

Of course the Germans attached to Barbarossa a legend, as they do to everything. They said that he was not dead, but had fallen a victim to enchantment. He and his knights had been put to sleep in the Kyffhauser cave in Thuringia. They sat around a stone table, waiting for release. His once red, but now white, beard was growing through the stone.

They also said that the spell that bound Barbarossa and his knights would some day be broken, and that they would come back to Germany. This would occur when the country should be in sore distress, and need a champion for its cause.

Ravens flew continually about the cave where the monarch and his knights were held enchanted. When they should cease to circle about it, the spell would be broken, and the grand old monarch would return to the Rhine.

They looked for him in days of calamity; but centuries passed, and he did not return.

The legend is thus told in song: —

"The ancient Barbarossa
By magic spell is bound, —
Old Frederick the Kaiser,
In castle underground.

"The Kaiser hath not perished,
He sleeps an iron sleep;
For, in the castle hidden,
He's sunk in slumber deep.

"With him the chiefest treasures
Of empire hath he ta'en,
Wherewith, in fitting season,
He shall appear again.

"The Kaiser he is sitting
Upon an ivory throne;
Of marble is the table
His head he resteth on.

"His beard it is not flaxen;
Like living fire it shines,
And groweth through the table
Whereon his chin reclines.

"As in a dream he noddeth,
Then wakes he, heavy-eyed,
And calls, with lifted finger,
A stripling to his side.

"'Dwarf, get thee to the gateway,
And tidings bring, if still
Their course the ancient ravens
Are wheeling round the hill.

"'For if the ancient ravens
Are flying still around,
A hundred years to slumber
By magic spell I 'm bound.'"
FRIEDRICH RÜCKERT.

The seven evenings with historic places on the Rhine had proved a source of profitable entertainment to the Club. It was proposed to continue the plan, and to follow Mr. Beal's and the boys' journey to the North.

"Let us add to these entertainments," said Charlie Leland,—

"(1) A Night in Northern Germany. We will call it a Hamburg Night.

"(2) A Night in Denmark.

"(3) A Night in Sweden and Norway."

The proposal was adopted, and Master Beal was asked to continue the narrative of travel, and all the members of the Club were requested to collect stories that illustrate the history, traditions, manners, and customs of these countries.

CHAPTER XII.

HAMBURG.

HAMBURG. — BERLIN. — POTSDAM. — PALACE OF SANS-SOUCI. — STORY OF THE STRUGGLES AND TRIUMPHS OF HANDEL. — STORY OF PETER THE WILD BOY.

HAMBURG, the fine old city of the Elbe, is almost as large as was Boston before the annexation; it is familiar by name to American ears, for it is from Hamburg, as a port, that the yearly army of German emigrants come.

"I looked sadly upon Hamburg as I thought how many eyes filled with tears had turned back upon her spires and towers, her receding harbor, and seen the Germany of their ancestors, and the old city of Charlemagne, with its historic associations of a thousand years, fade forever from view. Down the Elbe go the steamers, and the emigrants with their eyes fixed on the shores! Then westward, ho, for the prairie territories of the great empire of the New World!

"More than six thousand vessels enter the harbor of Hamburg in a year. The flags of all nations float there, but the British red is everywhere seen.

"We visited the church of St. Michael, and ascended the steeple, which is four hundred and thirty-two feet high, or one hundred feet higher than the spire of St. Paul's in London. We looked down on the city, the harbor, the canals. Our eye followed the Elbe on its way to the sea. On the north was Holstein; on the south, Hanover.

CANAL IN HAMBURG.

"From Hamburg we made a zigzag to Berlin and Potsdam. The railroad between the great German port and the brilliant capital is across a level country, the distance being about one hundred and seventy-five miles, or seven hours' ride.

"Berlin, capital of Prussia and of the German Empire, the residence of the German Emperor, is situated in the midst of a vast plain; 'an oasis of stone and brick in a Sahara of sand.' It is about the size of New York, and it greatly resembles an American city, for the reason that everything there seems new.

"It has been called a city of palaces, and so it is, for many of the private residences would be fitting abodes for kings. The architecture is everywhere beautiful; all the elegances of Greek art meet the eye wherever it may turn. Ruins there are none; old quarters, none; quaint Gothic or mediæval buildings, none. The streets are so regular, the public squares so artistic, and the buildings such models of art, that the whole becomes monotonous.

"'This is America over again,' said an American traveller, who had joined our party. 'Let us return.'

"Many of the buildings might remind one of the hanging gardens of old, so full are the balconies of flowers. The fronts of some of the private residences are flower gardens from the ground to the roofs.

"The emperor's palace is the crowning architectural glory of the city. It is four hundred feet long.

"We visited the Zoölogical Gardens and the National Gallery of Pictures, the entrance to which makes a beautiful picture.

"We rode to Potsdam, a distance of some twenty miles. Potsdam is the Versailles of Germany. The road to Potsdam is a continuous avenue of trees, like the roads near Boston.

"Of course our object in visiting the town was to see the palace and gardens of Sans-Souci, the favorite residence of Frederick the Great.

"Frederick loved everything that was French in art. The French expression is seen on everything at Sans-Souci. The approach to the

THE PALACE IN BERLIN.

palace is by an avenue through gardens laid out in the Louis Quatorze style, with alleys, hedges, statues, and fountains.

"The famous palace stands on the top flight of a series of broad terraces, fronted with glass. Beneath these terraces grow vines, olives, and orange-trees. In the rear of the palace is a colonnade. There Frederick used to pace to and fro in the sunshine, when failing health

GROTTO.

and old age admonished him that death was near. As his religious hopes were few, his reflections must have been rather lonely when death's winter came stealing on.

"The room where Frederick studied, and the adjoining apartment where he died, are shown. The former contains a library consisting wholly of books in French.

"We returned to Hamburg.

"We were in old Danish territory already. We stopped but one night at Hamburg on our return; then we made our way to the steamer which was to take us to the Denmark of to-day, Copenhagen."

Among the stories on the Hamburg Night was one by a music-loving student of Yule, which he called

THE CITY OF HANDEL'S YOUTH.

The composer of the "Messiah," George Frederick Handel, was born at Halle, Germany, Feb. 23, 1685. He sang before he could talk plainly. His father, a physician, was alarmed, for he had a poor opinion of music and musicians. As the child grew, nature asserted that he would be a musician; the father declared he should be a lawyer.

Little George was kept from the public school, because the gamut was there taught. He might go to no place where music would be heard, and no musical instrument was permitted in the house.

But nature, aided by the wiser mother, triumphed. In those days musical nuns played upon a dumb spinet, that they might not disturb the quiet of their convents. It was a sort of piano, and the strings were muffled with cloth. One of these spinets was smuggled into the garret of Dr. Handel's house. At night, George would steal up to the attic and practise upon it. But not a tinkle could the watchful father hear. Before the child was seven years of age he had taught himself to play upon the dumb instrument.

One day Dr. Handel started to visit a son in the service of a German duke. George begged to go, as he wished to hear the organ in the duke's chapel. But not until he ran after the coach did the father consent.

They arrived at the palace as a chapel service was going on. The boy stole away to the organ-loft, and, after service, begán playing. The duke, recognizing that it was not his organist's style, sent a servant to learn who was playing. The man returned with the trembling boy.

Dr. Handel was both amazed and enraged. But the duke, patting the child on the head, drew out his story. "You are stifling a genius," he said to the angry father; "this boy must not be snubbed." The doctor, more subservient to a prince than to nature, consented that his son should study music.

During three years the boy studied with Zachau, the organist of the Halle Cathedral. They were years of hard work. One day his teacher said to George, "I can teach you no longer; you already know more than I do. You must go

SANS-SOUCI.

and study in Berlin." Berlin was at once attracted to the youthful musician by his playing on the harpsichord and the organ. But the death of his father compelled him to earn his daily bread. Willing to descend, that he might rise, he became a violin player of minor parts at the Hamburg Opera House. The homage he had received prompted his vanity to create a surprise. He played badly, and acted as a verdant youth. The members of the orchestra sneeringly informed him that he would never earn his salt. Handel, however, waited his opportunity. One day the harpsichordist, the principal person in the orchestra, was absent. The band, thinking it would be a good joke, persuaded Handel to take his place. Laying aside his violin, he seated himself at the harpsichord, amid the smiles of the musicians. As he touched the keys the smiles gave place to looks of wonder. He played on, and the whole orchestra broke into loud applause. From that day until he left Hamburg, the youth of nineteen led the band.

Handel's extraordinary skill as a performer was not wholly due to genius. He practised incessantly, so that every key of his harpsichord was hollowed like a spoon.

Handel's greatest triumphs, as a composer, were won in England. But the music-loving Irish of Dublin had the honor of first welcoming his masterpiece, the "Messiah." Such was the enthusiasm it created that ladies left their hoops at home, in order to get one hundred more listeners into the room.

A German poet calls the "Messiah" "a Christian epic in musical sounds." The expression is a felicitous description of its theme and style. It celebrates the grandest of events with the sublimest strains that music may utter. The great composer commanded, and all the powers of music hastened with song and instrument to praise the life, death, and triumph of the Christ. No human composition ever voiced, in poetry or prose or music, such a masterly conception of the Virgin's Son as that uttered by this magnificent oratorio.

The sacred Scriptures furnish the words. The seer's prophecies, the Psalmist's strains, the evangelist's narrative, the angels' song, the anthem of the redeemed, are transferred to aria, recitative, and chorus. The sentiment is as majestic as the music is grand. He who sought out the fitting words had studied his Bible, and he who joined to them musical sounds dwelt in the region of the sublime.

All the emotions are touched by the oratorio. Words and music quiver with fear, utter sorrow, plead with pathos, or exult in the joy of triumph. A symphony so paints a pastoral scene that the shepherds of Bethlehem are seen watching their flocks. One air, "He was despised," suggests that its birth was amid tears. It was; for Handel sobbed aloud while composing it. It is the threnody of the oratorio.

The grandeur of the "Messiah" finds its highest expression in the "Hallelujah Chorus." "I did think," said Handel, describing, in imperfect English, his thought at the moment of composition, — "I did think I did see all heaven before me, and the great God himself."

When the oratorio was first performed in London, the audience were transported at the words, "The Lord God omnipotent reigneth." They all, with George II., who happened to be present, started to their feet and remained standing until the chorus was ended. This act of homage has become the custom with all English-speaking audiences.

"You have given the audience an excellent entertainment," said a patronizing nobleman to Handel, at the close of the first performance of the "Messiah" in London.

"My lord," replied the grand old composer, with dignity, "I should be very sorry if I only *entertained* them; I wish to make them *better.*"

A few years before his death Handel was smitten with blindness. He continued, however, to preside at his oratorios, being led by a lad to the organ, which, as leader, he played. One day, while conducting his oratorio of "Samson," the old man turned pale and trembled with emotion, as the bass sung the blind giant's lament: "Total eclipse! no sun, no moon!" As the audience saw the sightless eyes turned towards them, they were affected to tears.

Seized by a mortal illness, Handel expressed a wish that he might die on Good Friday, "in hope of meeting his good God, his sweet Lord and Saviour, on the day of his resurrection." This consolation, it seems, was not denied him. For on his monument, standing in the Poets' Corner of Westminster Abbey, is inscribed : "Died on Good Friday, April 14, 1759."

Another story, which is associated with the woods of Hanover, near Hamburg, was entitled

PETER THE WILD BOY.

In the year 1725, a few years after the capture of Marie le Blanc, a celebrated wild girl in France, there was seen in the woods, some twenty-five miles from Hanover, an object in form like a boy, yet running on his hands and feet, and eating grass and moss, like a beast.

The remarkable creature was captured, and was taken to Hanover by the superintendent of the House of Correction at Zell. It proved to be a boy evidently about thirteen years of age, yet possessing the habits and appetites of a mere animal. He was presented to King George I., at a state dinner at Hanover, and, the curiosity of the king being greatly excited, he became his patron.

In about a year after his capture he was taken to England, and exhibited to the court. While in that country he received the name of Peter the Wild Boy, by which ever after he was known.

Marie le Blanc, after proper training, became a lively, brilliant girl, and

PETER THE WILD BOY.

related to her friends and patrons the history of her early life; but Peter the Wild Boy seems to have been mentally deficient.

Dr. Arbuthnot, at whose house he resided for a time in his youth, spared no pains to teach him to talk; but his efforts met with but little success.

Peter seemed to comprehend the language and signs of beasts and birds far better than those of human beings, and to have more sympathy with the brute creation than with mankind. He, however, at last was taught to articulate the name of his royal patron, his own name, and some other words.

It was a long time before he became accustomed to the habits of civilization. He had evidently been used to sleeping on the boughs of trees, as a security from wild beasts, and when put to bed would tear the clothes, and hopping up take his naps in the corner of the room.

He regarded clothing with aversion, and when fully dressed was as uneasy as a culprit in prison. He was, however, generally docile, and submitted to discipline, and by degrees became more fit for human society.

He was attracted by beauty, and fond of finery, and it is related of him that he attempted to kiss the young and dashing Lady Walpole, in the circle at court. The manner in which the lovely woman received his attentions may be fancied.

Finding that he was incapable of education, his royal patron placed him in charge of a farmer, where he lived many years. Here he was visited by Lord Monboddo, a speculative English writer, who, in a metaphysical work, gives the following interesting account: —

"It was in the beginning of June, 1782, that I saw him in a farmhouse called Broadway, about a mile from Berkhamstead, kept there on a pension of thirty pounds, which the king pays. He is but of low stature, not exceeding five feet three inches, and though he must now be about seventy years of age, he has a fresh, healthy look. He wears his beard; his face is not at all ugly or disagreeable, and he has a look that may be called sensible or sagacious for a savage.

"About twenty years ago he used to elope, and once, as I was told, he wandered as far as Norfolk; but of late he has become quite tame, and either keeps the house or saunters about the farm. He has been, during the last thirteen years, where he lives at present, and before that he was twelve years with another farmer, whom I saw and conversed with.

"This farmer told me he had been put to school somewhere in Hertfordshire, but had only learned to articulate his own name, Peter, and the name of King George, both which I heard him pronounce very distinctly. But the woman of the house where he now is — for the man happened not to be home — told me he understood everything that was said to him concerning the common affairs of life, and I saw that he readily understood several things she said to him while I was present. Among other things she desired him to sing 'Nancy Dawson,' which he accordingly did, and another tune that she named. He was never mischievous, but had that gentleness of manners which I hold to be characteristic of our nature, at least till we become carnivorous, and hunters, or warriors. He feeds at present as the farmer and his wife do; but, as I was told by an old woman who remembered to have seen him when he first came to Hertfordshire, which she computed to be about fifty-five years before, he then fed much on leaves, particularly of cabbage, which she saw him eat raw. He was then, as she thought, about fifteen years of age, walked upright, but could climb trees like a squirrel. At present he not only eats flesh, but has acquired a taste for beer, and even for spirits, of which he inclines to drink more than he can get.

"The old farmer with whom he lived before he came to his present situation informed me that Peter had that taste before he came to him. He has also become very fond of fire, but has not acquired a liking for money; for though he takes it he does not keep it, but gives it to his landlord or landlady, which I suppose is a lesson they have taught him. He retains so much of his natural instinct that he has a fore-feeling of bad weather, growling, and howling, and showing great disorder before it comes on."

Another philosopher, who made him a visit, obtained the following luminous information: —

"Who is your father?"
"King George."
"What is your name?"
"Pe-ter."
"What is *that*?" (pointing to a dog.)
"Bow-wow."
"What are you?"
"Wild man."
"Where were you found?"
"Hanover."
"Who found you?"
"King George."

About the year 1746 he ran away, and, entering Scotland, was arrested as an English spy. His captors endeavored to force from him some terrible disclosure, but could obtain nothing, not even an answer, and it was something of a puzzle to them to determine exactly what they had captured.

They at last resolved to inflict punishment upon him for his obstinacy, but were deterred by a lady who recognized him and disclosed his history.

In his latter years he made himself useful to the farmer with whom he lived, but he required constant watchfulness, else he would make grave blunders. An amusing anecdote is told of his manner of working when left to himself.

He was required, during the absence of his guardian, to fill a cart with compost, which he did ; but, having filled the cart in the usual way, and finding himself out of employment, he directly shovelled the compost out again, and when the farmer returned the cart was empty.

But poor Peter, with all his dulness, possessed some remarkable characteristics. He was very strong of arm, and wonderfully swift of foot, and his senses were acute. His musical gifts were most marvellous. He would reproduce, in his humming way, the notes of a tune that he had heard but once, — a thing that might have baffled an amateur.

He also had a lively sense of the beautiful and the sublime. He would stand at night gazing on the stars as though transfixed by the splendors blazing above. His whole being was thrilled with joy on the approach of spring. He would sing all the day as the atmosphere became warm and balmy; and would often prolong his melodies far into the beautiful nights.

He died aged about seventy years.

CHAPTER XIII.

THE BELLS OF THE RHINE.

LEGENDS OF THE BELLS OF BASEL AND SPEYER. — STORY OF THE HARMONY CHIME. —
THE BELL-FOUNDER OF BRESLAU.

NE evening, after the story-telling entertainments, Mr. Beal was speaking to the Class of the great bell of Cologne which has been cast from the French cannon captured in the last war.

"It seems a beautiful thing," he said, "that the guns of war should be made to ring out the notes of peace."

"There is one subject that we did not treat at our meetings," said Charlie Leland, — "the bells of the Rhine."

"True," said Mr. Beal. "A volume might be written on the subject. Almost every belfry on the Rhine has its legend, and many of them are associated with thrilling events of history. The raftmen, as they drift down the river on the Sabbath, associate almost every bell they hear with a story. The bells of Basle (Basel), Strasburg, Speyer, Heidelberg, Worms, Frankfort, Mayence, Bingen, and Bonn all ring out a meaning to the German student that the ordinary traveller does not comprehend. Bell land is one of mystery.

"For example, the clocks of Basel. The American traveller arrives at Basel, and hurries out of his hotel, and along the beautiful public gardens, to the terrace overlooking the Rhine. He looks down on the picturesque banks of the winding river; then far away his eye seeks the peaks of the Jura.

"The bells strike. The music to his ears has no history.

"The German and French students hear them with different ears. The old struggles of Alsace and Romaine come back to memory. They recall the fact that the city was once saved by a heroic watchman, who confused the enemy by causing the bells to strike the wrong hour. To continue the memory of this event, the great bell of Basel during the Middle Ages was made to strike the hour of one at noonday.

"The bells of Speyer have an interesting legend. Henry IV. was one of the most unfortunate men who ever sat upon a throne. His own son, afterward Henry V., conspired against him, and the Pope declared him an outlaw.

"Deserted by every one, he went into exile, and made his home at Ingleheim, on the Rhine. One old servant, Kurt, followed his changing fortunes. He died at Liege.

"Misfortune followed the once mighty emperor even after death. The Pope would not allow his body to be buried for several years. Kurt watched by the coffin, like Rizpah by the bodies of her sons. He made it his shrine: he prayed by it daily.

"At last the Pope consented that the remains of the emperor should rest in the earth. The body was brought to Speyer. Kurt followed it. It was buried with great pomp, and tollings of bells.

"Some months after the ceremonious event Kurt died. As his breath was passing, say the legendary writers, all the bells began to toll. The bellmen ran to the belfries; no one was there, but the bells tolled on, swayed, it was believed, by unseen hands.

"Henry V. died in the same town. He was despised by the people, and he suffered terrible agonies in his last hours. As his last moments came the bells began to toll again. It was not the usual announcement of the death of the good, but the sharp notes that proclaim that a criminal is being led to justice; at least, so the people came to believe.

THE SILENT CASTLES.

"One of the most beautiful stories of bells that I ever met is associated with a once famous factory that cast some of the most melodious bells in Holland and the towns of the Rhine. I will tell it to you.

THE HARMONY CHIME.

Many years ago, in a large iron foundry in the city of Ghent, was found a young workman by the name of Otto Holstein. He was not nineteen years of age, but none of the workmen could equal him in his special department, — bell

HOTEL DE VILLE, GHENT.

casting or moulding. Far and near the fame of Otto's bells extended, — the clearest and sweetest, people said, that were ever heard.

Of course the great establishment of Von Erlangen, in which Otto worked, got the credit of his labors; but Von Erlangen and Otto himself knew very well to whom the superior tone of the bells was due. The master did not pay him higher wages than the others, but by degrees he grew to be general superintendent in his department in spite of his extreme youth.

"Yes, my bells are good," he said to a friend one day, who was commenting upon their merits; "but they do not make the music I will yet strike from them. They ring alike for all things. To be sure, when they toll for a funeral the slow measure makes them *seem* mournful, but then the notes are really the same as in a wedding peal. I shall make a chime of bells that will sound at will every chord in the human soul."

"Then wilt thou deal in magic," said his friend, laughing; "and the Holy Inquisition will have somewhat to do with thee. No human power can turn a bell into a musical instrument."

"But I can," he answered briefly; "and, Inquisition or not, I will do it."

He turned abruptly from his friend and sauntered, lost in thought, down the narrow street which led to his home. It was an humble, red-tiled cottage, of only two rooms, that he had inherited from his grandfather. There he lived alone with his widowed mother. She was a mild, pleasant-faced woman, and her eyes brightened as her son bent his tall head under the low doorway, as he entered the little room. "Thou art late, Otto," she said, "and in trouble, too," as she caught sight of his grave, sad face.

"Yes," he answered. "When I asked Herr Erlangen for an increase of salary, for my work grows harder every day, he refused it. Nay, he told me if I was not satisfied, I could leave, for there were fifty men ready to take my place. Ready! yes, I warrant they're ready enough, but to be *able* is a different thing."

His mother sighed deeply.

"Thou wilt not leave Herr Erlangen's, surely. It is little we get, but it keeps us in food."

"I must leave," he answered. "Nay, do not cry out, mother! I have other plans, and thou wilt not starve. Monsieur Dayrolles, the rich Frenchman, who lives in the Linden-Strasse, has often asked me why I do not set up a foundry of my own. Of course I laughed, — I, who never have a thaler to spend; but he told me he and several other rich friends of his would advance the means to start me in business. He is a great deal of his time at Erlangen's, and is an enthusiast about fine bells. Ah! we are great friends, and I am going to him after supper."

"People say he is crazy," said his mother.

"Crazy!" indignantly. "People say that of everybody who has ideas they can't understand. They say *I* am crazy when I talk of my chime of bells. If I stay with Erlangen, he gets the credit of my work; but my chime must be mine, — mine alone, mother." His eyes lighted with a kind of wild enthusiasm whenever he talked on this subject.

His mother's cheerful face grew sad, as she laid her hand on his shoulder.

"Why, Otto, thou art not thyself when thou speakest of those bells."

"More my real self, mother, than at any other time!" he cried. "I only truly live when I think of how my idea is to be carried out. It is to be my life's work; I know it, I feel it. It is upon me that my fate is woven inextricably in that ideal chime. It is God-sent. No great work, but the maker is possessed wholly by it. Don't shake your head, mother. Wait till my 'Harmony Chime' sounds from the great cathedral belfry, and then shake it if you can."

His mother smiled faintly.

"Thou art a boy, — a mere child, Otto, though a wonderful genius, I must confess. Thy hopes delude thee, for it would take a lifetime to carry out thine idea."

"Then let it take a lifetime!" he cried out vehemently. "Let me accomplish it when I am too old to hear it distinctly, and I will be content that its first sounds toll my dirge. I must go now to Monsieur Dayrolles. Wish me good luck, dearest mother." And he stooped and kissed her tenderly.

Otto did not fail. The strange old man in his visits to the foundry had noticed the germs of genius in the boy, and grown very fond of him. He was so frank, so honest, so devoted to his work, and had accomplished so much at his early age, that Monsieur Dayrolles saw a brilliant future before him. Besides, the old gentleman, with a Frenchman's vanity, felt that if the "Harmony Chime" *could* be made, the name of the munificent patron would go down to posterity with that of the maker. He believed firmly that the boy would some day accomplish his purpose. So, although the revolt of the Netherlands had begun and he was preparing to return to his own country, he advanced the necessary funds, and saw Otto established in business before he quitted Ghent.

In a very short time work poured in upon Otto. During that long and terrible war the manufacture of cannon alone made the fortunes of the workers in iron. So five years from the time he left Von Erlangen we find Otto Holstein a rich man at twenty-four years of age. But the idea for which he labored had never for a moment left his mind. Sleeping or waking, toiling or resting, his thoughts were busy perfecting the details of the great work.

"Thou art twenty-four to-day, Otto," said his good mother, "and rich beyond our hopes. When wilt thou bring Gertrude home to me? Thou hast been betrothed now for three years, and I want a daughter to comfort my declining years. Thou doest thy betrothed maiden a grievous wrong to delay without cause. The gossips are talking already."

"Let them talk," laughed Otto. "Little do Gertrude or I care for their silly tongues. She and I have agreed that the 'Harmony Chime' is to usher in our marriage-day. Why, good mother, no man can serve two mistresses, and my chime has the oldest claim. Let me accomplish it, and then the remainder of my life belongs to Gertrude, and thou, too, best of mothers."

"Still that dream! still that dream!" sighed his mother. "Thou hast cast bell after bell, and until to-day I have heard nothing more of the wild idea."

"No, because I needed money. I needed time, and thought, too, to make experiments. All is matured now. I have received an order to make a new set of bells for the great cathedral that was sacked last week by the 'Iconoclasts,' and I begin to-morrow."

BELL-TOWER, GHENT.

As Otto had said, his life's work began the next day. He loved his mother, but he seemed now to forget her in the feverish eagerness with which he threw himself into his labors. He had been a devoted lover to Gertrude, but he now never had a spare moment to give to her, — in fact, he only seemed to remember her existence in connection with the peal which would ring in their wedding-day. His labors were prolonged far over the appointed time, and meanwhile the internal war raged more furiously, and the Netherlands were one vast battle-field. No interest did Otto seem to take in the stirring events around him. The bells held his whole existence captive.

BELL TOWER OF HEIDELBERG.

At last the moulds were broken, and the bells came out of their husks perfect in form, and shining as stars in Otto's happy eyes. They were mounted in the great belfry, and for the test-chime Otto had employed the best bell-ringers in the city.

It was a lovely May morning; and, almost crazed with excitement and anxiety, Otto, accompanied by a few chosen friends, waited outside the city for the first notes of the Harmony Chime. At some distance he thought he could better judge of the merits of his work.

At last the first notes were struck, clear, sonorous, and so melodious that his friends cried aloud with delight. But with finger upraised for silence, and eyes full of ecstatic delight, Otto stood like a statue until the last note died away. Then his friends caught him as he fell forward in a swoon, — a swoon so like death that no one thought he would recover.

But it was not death, and he came out of it with a look of serene peace on his face that it had not worn since boyhood. He was married to Gertrude that very day, but every one noticed that the ecstasy which transfigured his face seemed to be drawn more from the sound of the bells than the sweet face beside him.

"Don't you see a spell is cast on him as soon as they begin to ring?" said one, after the bells had ceased to be a wonder. "If he is walking, he stops short, and if he is working, the work drops and a strange fire comes in his eyes; and I have seen him shudder all over as if he had an ague."

In good truth, the bells seemed to have drawn a portion of Otto's life to them. When the incursions of the war forced him to fly from Ghent with his family, his regrets were not for his injured property, but that he could not hear the bells.

He was absent two years, and when he returned it was to find the cathedral almost a ruin, and the bells gone no one knew where. From that moment a settled melancholy took possession of Otto. He made no attempt to retrieve his losses; in fact, he gave up work altogether, and would sit all day with his eyes fixed on the ruined belfry.

People said he was melancholy mad, and I suppose it was the truth; but he was mad with a kind of gentle patience very sad to see. His mother had died during their exile, and now his wife, unable with all her love to rouse him from his torpor, faded slowly away. He did not notice her sickness, and his poor numbed brain seemed imperfectly to comprehend her death. But he followed her to the grave, and turning from it moved slowly down the city, passed the door of his old home without looking at it, and went out of the city gates.

After that he was seen in every city in Europe at different intervals. Charitable people gave him alms, but he never begged. He would enter a town, take his station near a church and wait until the bells rang for matins or vespers, then take up his staff and, sighing deeply, move off. People noting the wistful look in his eyes would ask him what he wanted.

"I am seeking, — I am seeking," was his only reply; and those were almost the only words any one ever heard from him, and he muttered them often to himself. Years rolled over the head of the wanderer, but still his slow march from town to town continued. His hair had grown white, and his strength had failed him so much that he only tottered instead of walked, but still that wistful seeking look was in his eyes.

He heard the old bells on the Rhine in his wanderings. He lingered long near the belfries of the sweetest voices; but their melodious tongues only spoke to him of his lost hope.

He left the river of sweet bells, and made a pilgrimage to England. It was the days of cathedrals in their beauty and glory, and here he again heard the tones that he loved, but which failed to realize his own ideal.

When a person fails to fulfil his ideal, his whole life seems a failure, — like something glorious and beautiful one meets and loses, and never again finds.

"Be true to the dreams of thy youth," says a German author; and every soul is unhappy until the dreams of youth prove true.

One glorious evening in midsummer Otto was crossing a river in Ireland. The kind-hearted boatman had been moved by the old man's imploring gestures to cross him. "He's mighty nigh his end, anyhow," he muttered, looking at the feeble movements of the old pilgrim as he stumbled to his seat.

Suddenly through the still evening air came the distant sound of a melodious chime. At the first note the pilgrim leaped to his feet and threw up his arms.

"O my God," he cried, "found at last!"

"It's the bells of the Convent," said the wondering man, not understanding Otto's words spoken in a foreign tongue, but answering his gesture. "They was brought from somewhere in Holland when they were fighting there. Moighty fine bells they are, anyhow. But he is n't listening to me."

No, he heard nothing but the bells. He merely whispered, "Come back to me after so many years, — O love of my soul, O thought of my life! Peal on, for your voices tell me of Paradise."

The last note floated through the air, and as it died away something else soared aloft forever, free from the clouds and struggles of life.

BRESLAU.

His ideal was fulfilled now. Otto lay dead, his face full of peace and joy, for the weary quest of his crazy brain was over, and the Harmony Chime had called him to his eternal rest.

And, past that change of life that men call Death, we may well believe that he heard in the ascension to the celestial atmosphere the ringing of welcoming bells more beautiful than the Harmony Chime.

"I will relate another story," said Mr. Beal. "It is like the Harmony Chime, but has a sadder ending."

THE BELL-FOUNDER OF BRESLAU.

THERE once lived in Breslau a famous bell-founder, the fame of whose skill caused his bells to be placed in many German towers. According to the ballad of Wilhelm Müller, —

> "And all his bells they sounded
> So full and clear and pure :
> He poured his faith and love in,
> Of that all men were sure.
> But of all bells that ever
> He cast, was one the crown,
> That was the bell for sinners
> At Breslau in the town."

He had an ambition to cast one bell that would surpass all others in purity of tone, and that should render his own name immortal.

He was required to cast a bell for the Magdalen Church tower of that city of noble churches, — Breslau. He felt that this was opportunity for his masterpiece. All of his thoughts centred on the Magdalen bell.

After a long period of preparation, his metals were arranged for use. The form was walled up and made steady; the melting of the metals in the great bell-kettle had begun.

The old bell-founder had two faults which had grown upon him; a love of ale and a fiery temper.

While the metals were heating in the kettle, he said to his fire-watch, a little boy, —

"Tend the kettle for a moment; I am overwrought: I must go over to the inn, and take my ale, and nerve me for the casting.

"But, boy," he added, "touch not the stopple; if you do, you shall rue it.

FINISHING THE BELL.

That bell is my life, I have put all I have learned in life into it. If any man were to touch that stopple, I would strike him dead."

AT THE INN.

The boy had an over-sensitive, nervous temperament. He was easily excited, and was subject to impulses that he could not easily control.

The command that he should not touch the stopple, under the dreadful penalty, strongly affected his mind, and made him wish to do the very thing he had been forbidden.

He watched the metal in the great kettle. It bubbled, billowed, and ran to and fro. In the composition of the glowing mass he knew that his master had put his heart and soul.

It would be a bold thing to touch the stopple,—adventurous. His hand began to move towards it.

The evil impulse grew, and his hand moved on.

He touched the stopple. The impulse was a wild passion now,— he turned it.

Then his mind grew dark — he was filled with horror.. He ran to his master.

"I have turned the stopple; I could not help it," he said. "The Devil tempted me!"

The old bell-founder clasped his hands and looked upward in agony. Then his temper flashed over him. He seized his knife, and stabbed the boy to the heart.

He rushed back to the foundry, hoping to stay the stream. He found the metal whole; the turning of the stopple had not caused the metal to flow.

The boy lay dead on the ground.

The old bell-founder knew the consequences of his act, and he did not seek to escape them. He cast

THE DAY OF EXECUTION.

the bell; then he went to the magistrates, and said,—

"My work is done; but I am a murderer. Do with me as you will."

The trial was short; it greatly excited the city. The judges could not do otherwise than sentence him to death. But as he was penitent, he was promised that on the day of his execution he should receive the offices and consolations of the Church.

"You are good," he said. "But grant me another favor. My bells will delight many ears when I am gone; my soul is in them; grant me another favor."

"Name it," said the judges.

"That I may hear the sound of my new bell before I die."

The judges consulted, and answered, —

"It shall toll for your execution."

The fatal day came.

Toll, toll, toll!

There was a sadness in the tone of the bell that touched every heart in Breslau. The bell seemed human.

. Toll, toll, toll!

How melodious! how perfect! how beautiful! The very air seemed charmed! The years would come and go, and this bell would be the tongue of Breslau!

The old man came forth. He had forgotten his fate in listening to the bell. The heavy clang was so melodious that it filled his heart with joy.

"That is it! that is it; my heart, my life!" he said. "I know all the metals; I made the voice! Ring on, ring on forever! Ring in holy days, and happy festivals, and joy eternal to Breslau."

Toll, toll, toll!

On passed the white-haired man, listening still to the call of the bell that summoned him to death.

He bowed his head at the place of execution to meet the stroke just as the last tone of the bell melted upon the air. His soul passed amid the silvery echoes. The bell rings on.

> "Ay, of all bells that ever
> He cast, is this the crown,
> The bell of Church St. Magdalen
> At Breslau in the town.
> It was, from that time forward,
> Baptized the Sinner's Bell;
> Whether it still is called so,
> Is more than I can tell."

"There is a sadness in the bells of the Rhine," continued Mr. Beal, "as they ring from old belfries at evening under the ruins of the castles on the hills. The lords of the Rhine that once heard them are gone forever. The vineyards creep up the hills on the light trellises, and the sun and the earth, as it were, fill the grapes with wine. The woods are as green as of old. The rafts go drifting down the light waves as on feet of air. But the river of history is changed, and one feels the spirit of the change with deep sadness as one listens to the bells."

THE LIGHTS HAVE GONE OUT IN THE CASTLE.

I.

The boatmen strike lightly the zither
As they drift 'neath the hillsides of green,
But gone from the Rhine is the palgrave,
And gone is the palgravine.
  Play lightly, play lightly, O boatman,
    When the shadows of night round thee fall,
  For the lights have gone out in the castle,
    The lights have gone out in the hall.
  And the Rhine waters silently flow,
  The old bells ring solemn and slow,
    O boatman,
      Play lightly,
        Play lightly,
  O boatman, play lightly and low.

II.

Awake the old runes on the zither,
O boatman! the lips of the Rhine
Still kiss the green ruins of ivy,
And smile on the vineyards of wine.
  Play lightly, play lightly, O boatman,
    When the shadows of night round thee fall,
  For the lights have gone out in the castle,
    The lights have gone out in the hall.
  And the Rhine waters silently flow,
  The old bells ring solemn and slow,
    O boatman,
      Play lightly,
        Play lightly,
  O boatman, play lightly and low.

ABOVE THE TOWN.

III.

The lamps of the stars shine above thee
As they shone when the vineyards were green,
In the long vanished days of the palgrave,
In the days of the palgravine.
Play lightly, thy life tides are flowing,
Thy fate in the palgrave's recall,
For the lights have gone out in the castle,
The lights have gone out in the hall.
And the Rhine waters silently flow,
And the old bells ring solemn and slow,
O boatman,
Play lightly,
Play lightly,
O boatman, play lightly and low.

The narratives of the evening devoted to the Bells on the Rhine were closed by a story by Master Lewis.

"I do not often relate stories," he said; "but I have a German story in mind, the lesson of which has been helpful to my experience. It is a legend and a superstition, and one that is not' as generally familiar to the readers of popular books as are many that have been told at these meetings. I think you will like it, and that you will not soon forget it."

"TO-MORROW."

ONCE — many years, perhaps centuries ago — a young German student, named Lek, was travelling from Leipsig to the Middle Rhine. His journey was made on foot, and a part of it lay through the Thuringian Forest.

He rested one night at the old walled town of Saalfeld, visited the ruins of Sorenburg, and entered one of the ancient roads then greatly frequented, but less used now, on account of the shorter and swifter avenues of travel.

Towards evening he ascended a hill, and, looking down, was surprised to discover a quaint town at the foot, of which he had never heard.

It was summer; the red sun was going down, and the tree-tops of the vast forests, moved by a gentle wind, seemed like the waves of the wide sea. Lek was a lover of the beautiful expressions of Nature, of the poetry of the forests, hills, and streams; and he sat down on a rock, under a spreading tree, to see the sunset flame and fade, and the far horizons sink into the shadows and disappear.

"I have made a good journey to-day," he said, "and whatever the strange town below me may be, it will be safe for me to spend the night there. I see that it has a church and an inn."

Lek had travelled much over Germany, but he had never before seen a town like the one below him. It wore an air of strange antiquity, — as a town might look that had remained unchanged for many hundred years. An old banner hung out from a quaint steepled building; but it was unlike any of modern times, national or provincial.

The fires of sunset died away; clouds, like smoke, rose above them, and a deep shadow overspread the forests. Lek gathered up his bundles, and descended the hill towards the town. As he was hurrying onward he met a strange-looking man in a primitive habit, — evidently a villager. Lek asked him the name of the place.

OLD PEASANT COSTUMES.

The stranger looked at him sadly and with surprise, and answered in a dialect that he did not wholly understand; but he guessed at the last words, and rightly.

"Why do you wish to know?"

"I am a traveller," answered Lek, "and I must remain there until to-morrow."

"To-morrow!" said the man, throwing up his hands. "To-morrow! For *us*," pointing to himself, "there is no to-morrow. I must hurry on."

He strode away towards a faded cottage on the outskirts of the town, leaving Lek to wonder what his mysterious answer could mean.

Lek entered the town. The people were strange to him; every one seemed to be in a hurry. Men and women were talking rapidly, like travellers when taking leave of their friends for a long journey. Indeed, so earnest were their words that they seemed hardly to notice him at all.

He presently met an old woman on a crutch, hurrying along the shadowy street.

THE OLD CITY.

THE BELLS OF THE RHINE.

"Is this the way to the inn?" he asked.

The old one hobbled on. He followed her.

"Is this the way to the inn? I wish to remain there until to-morrow."

The cripple turned on her crutch.

"To-morrow!" she said. "Who are you that talk of to-morrow? All the gold of the mountains could not buy a to-morrow. Go back to your own, young man! they may have to-morrows; but my time is short, — I must hurry on."

Away hobbled the dame; and Lek, wondering at her answer, entered what seemed to him the principal street.

He came at length to the inn; a faded structure, and antique, like a picture of the times of old. There men were drinking and talking; men in gold lace, and with long purses filled with ancient coin.

The landlord was evidently a rich old fellow; he had a girdle of jewels, and was otherwise habited much like a king.

He stared at Lek; so did his jovial comrades.

"Can you give a stranger hospitality until to-morrow?" asked the young student, bowing.

"Until TO-MORROW! Ha, ha, ha!" laughed the innkeeper. "He asks for hospitality until to-morrow!" he added to his six jolly companions.

"To-morrow — ha, ha, ha!" echoed one.

"Ha, ha, ha!" repeated another.

"Ha, ha, ha!" chorused the others, slapping their hands on their knees. "To-morrow!"

Then a solemn look came into the landlord's face.

"Young man," said he, "don't you know, have you not heard? *We* have no to-morrows; our nights are long, long slumbers; each one is a hundred years."

OLD PEASANT COSTUME.

The six men were talking now, and the landlord turned from Lek and joined in the conversation eagerly.

The shadows of the long twilight deepened. Men and women ran to and fro in the streets. Every one seemed in a hurry, as though much must be said and done in a brief time.

Presently a great bell sounded in a steeple. The hurrying people paused. Each one uplifted his or her hands, waved them in a circle, and cried, —

"Alas! To-morrow! Hurry, good men, all, good women, all, hurry!"

What did it mean? "Have I gone mad?" asked Lek. "Am I dreaming?" Near the inn was a green, parched and faded. In the centre was a withered tree; under it was a maiden. She was very fair; her dress was of silk and jewels, and on her arms were heavy bracelets of gold. Unlike the other people, she did not seem hurried and anxious. She appeared to take little interest in the strangely stimulated activities around her.

Lek went to her.

"Pardon a poor student seeking information," he said. "Your people all treat me rudely and strangely; they will not listen to me. I am a traveller, and I came here civilly, and only asked for food and lodging until to-morrow."

"TO-MORROW! The word is a terror to most of them; it is no terror to me. I care not for to-morrows,— they are days of disappointments; I had them once,— I am glad they do not come oftener to me. I shall go to sleep at midnight, here where I was deserted. You are a stranger, I see. You belong to the world; every day has its to-morrow. Go away, away to your own people, and to your own life of to-morrows. This is no place for you here."

OLD PEASANT COSTUMES.

Again the bell sounded. The hurrying people stopped again in the street, and waved their hands wildly, and cried,—

"Haste, haste, good men, all, good women, all. The hour is near. Good men, all, good women, all, hurry!"

It was night now; but the full moon rose over the long line of hills, and behind it appeared a black cloud, from which darted tongues of red flame, followed by mutterings of thunder.

The moon ascended the clear sky like a chariot, and the cloud seemed to follow her like an army,— an awful spectacle that riveted Lek's gaze and made him apprehensive.

"A storm is coming," he said. "I must stay here. Tell me, good maiden, where can I find food and shelter?"

"Have you a true heart?"

"I have a true heart. I have always been true to myself; and he who is true to himself is never unfaithful to God or his fellow-men."

"Then you will be saved when the hour comes. They only go down with us who are untrue. All true hearts have to-morrows."

The moon ascended higher, and her light, more resplendent, heightened the effect of the blackness of the rising cloud. The lightnings became more vivid, the thunder more distinct.

CITY GATE.

"You are sure that your heart is true?" said the maiden.

"By the Cross, it is true."

"Then I have a duty to do. Follow me."

She rose and walked towards the hill from which Lek had come. Lek followed her. As he passed out of the town the bell sounded: it was the hour of eleven.

The people stopped in the streets as before, waving their hands, and crying,—

"Good men, all, good women, all, hurry! The hour is near. Good men, all, good women, all, hurry!"

The maiden ascended the hill to the very rock from which the student had first seen the town, and under which he had rested.

"Sit you here," she said, "and do not leave the place until the cocks crow for morning. A true heart never perished with the untrue. My duty is done. Farewell!"

"But the tempest?" said the student. "This is no place of shelter. Let me return with you, only until to-morrow."

There burst upon the hill a terrific thunder-gust. The maiden was gone, the black cloud swept over the moon, and Lek could no longer discern the town in the valley. Everything around him grew dark. The air seemed to turn into a thick inky darkness.

Fearful flashes of lightning and terrific thunder followed. The wind bent the forest before it; but not a drop of rain fell.

There was a moment's silence. The bell in the mysterious steeple smote upon the air. It was midnight.

Another hush, as though Nature had ceased to breathe. Then a thunder-crash shook the hills, and seemed to cleave open the very earth.

THE NECKAR

Lek crossed himself and fell upon his knees. The cloud passed swiftly. The moon came out again, revealing the lovely valley. *The village was gone.*

In the morning a cowherd came up the hill at the rising of the sun.

"Good morrow," said Lek. "That was a fearful tempest that we had at midnight."

"I never heard such thunder," said the cowherd. "I almost thought that the final day had come. You may well say it was a fearful night, my boy."

"But what has become of the village that was in the valley yesterday?" asked Lek.

"There is no village in the valley," said the cowherd. "There never was but one. That was sunk hundreds of years ago; if you saw any village there yesterday it was that: it comes up only once in a hundred years, and then it remains for only a single day. Woe betide the traveller that stops there *that* day. Unless he have a true heart, he goes down with the town at midnight.

The town was cursed because it waxed rich, and became so wicked that there was found in it but one heart that was true."

"Tell me about this strange village," said Lek, in fear and awe, recalling his adventure. "I never before heard of a thing so mysterious."

"It is a sorry story. I will tell it as I have heard it.

"The hills of Reichmanndorf used to abound with gold, and the people of the old town all became rich; but their riches did not make them happy and contented. It made them untrue.

"The more their wealth increased, the more unfaithful they became, until the men met in the market-place daily to defraud each other, and the women's only purpose in life was to display their vanity.

"At the inn were nightly carousals. The young men thought only of their gains and dissipations. Men were untrue to their families, and lovers to their vows.

"The Sabbath was not kept. The old priest, Van Ness, said masses to the empty aisles.

"In those evil days lived one Frederic Wollin. He was a brave man, and his soul was true.

"It was the custom of this good man to instruct the people in the market-place. But at last none came to hear him.

"One day, near Christmas, the council met. Wine flowed; rude jests went round. The question was discussed as to how these days of selfish delights might be made perpetual.

"A great cry arose:—

"'Banish the holy days: then all our to-morrows will be as to-day!'

"Then Wollin arose and faced the people. His appearance was met by a tumult, and his words increased the hatred long felt against him.

"'The days of evil have no to-morrows,' he said. 'He that liveth to himself is dead.'

"'Give him a holy day once in a hundred years!' cried one.

The voice was hailed with cheers. The council voted that all future days should be as that day, except that Wollin and the old priest, Van Ness, should have a holy day once in a hundred years.

"Christmas came. No bell was rung; no chant was heard. Easter brought flowers to the woods, but none to the altar. Purple Pentecost filled the forest villages with joy; but here no one cared to recall the descent of the celestial fire except the old priest and Wollin.

"It was such a night as last night when Van Ness and Wollin came out of the church for the last time. The people were drinking at the inn, and dancing upon the green. Spring was changing into deep summer; the land was filled with blooms.

"A party of young men who had been carousing, on seeing Wollin come from the church, set upon him, and compelled him to leave the town. He came up this hill. When he had reached the top, he paused and lifted his face towards heaven, and stretched out his hand. As he did so, a sharp sound rent the valley, and caused the hills to tremble. He looked down. The village had disappeared. Only Van Ness was standing by his side.

"But as the villagers had promised Wollin a holy day once in a hundred years, so once in a hundred years these people are permitted to rise with their village into the light of the sun for a single day. If on that day a stranger visits them whose heart is untrue he disappears with them at midnight. Such is the story. You will hardly believe it true."

The student crossed himself, and went on his journey towards the Rhine.

"*They* have one day in a hundred years," he said. "How precious must that one day be to them! If I enter the ways of evil, and my heart becomes untrue, shall *I* have *one* day in one hundred years when life is ended and my account to Heaven is rendered?"

He thought. He read the holy books. He tried to find a single hope for an untrue soul ; but he could discover none.

Then he said, —

"The days of evil have no to-morrows, — no, not once in a hundred years. Only good deeds have to-morrows. I will be true: so shall to-morrows open and close like golden doors until time is lost in the eternal." And his heart remained true.

CHAPTER XIV.

THE SONGS OF THE RHINE.

THE WATCHMAN'S SONG. — THE WILD HUNT OF LÜTZOW. — THE AUTHOR OF THE ERL
KING. — BEETHOVEN'S BOYHOOD. — THE ORGAN-TEMPEST OF LUCERNE.

HINELAND is the land of song. It is the wings of song that have given it its fame. Every town on the Rhine has its own songs; every mountain, hill, and river.

America has few local songs, — few songs of the people. The singers who give voices to rivers, lakes, mountains, and valleys have not yet appeared. The local poets and singers of America are yet to come.

In England, Germany, and some of the provinces of France, every temple, stream, and grove has had its sweet singer.

Go to Basle, and you may hear the clubs singing the heroic songs of Alsace and Lorraine.

Go to Heidelberg, and you may listen to student-songs through which breathe the national spirit of hundreds of years.

The bands tell the story, legend, or romance of such towns at night, wherever they may play.

In one of the public grounds to which the Class went for an evening rest, one of the bands was playing the *Fremersberg*.

It related an old romance of the region of Baden-Baden: how that a nobleman was once wandering with his dogs in the mountains, and was overtaken by a storm; how he was about to perish when he heard the distant sounds of a monastery bell; how, following the direction of the sound, he heard a chant of priests; and how, at last, he was saved.

The piece was full of melody. The wind, the rain, the horns, the bells, the chant, while they told a story, were all delightfully melodious.

The ballad is almost banished from the intellectual American concert-rooms. In Germany a ballad is a gem, and is so valued. It is the best expression of national life and feeling.

The Class went to hear one of Germany's greatest singers. She sang an heroic selection, and was recalled. Her first words on the recall hushed the audience: it was a ballad of the four stages of life. It began with an incident of a child dreaming under a rosebush: —

"Sweetly it sleeps and on dream wings flies
To play with the angels in Paradise,
And the years glide by."

as an English translation gives it.

In the last stanza, the child having passed through the stages of life, was represented as again sleeping under a rosebush. The withered leaves fall upon his grave.

"Withered and dead they fall to the ground,
And silently cover a new-made mound,
And the years glide by."

These last lines were rendered so softly, yet distinctly, that they seemed like tremulous sounds in the air. The singer's face hardly appeared to move; every listener was like a statue. The silence was almost painful and impressive. One could but feel this was indeed art, and not a pretentious affectation of it.

The reign of the organ as the monarch of musical instruments began with Charlemagne, and nearly all of the towns on the Rhine have historic organs. Many of the organ pieces are local composi-

AN OLD GERMAN TOWN.

tions and imitative. On the great organs at Basle and Frieburg the imitation of storms is sometimes produced.

None of these storm-pieces, however, equal that which is daily played in summer on the organ of Lucerne. This organ tempest more greatly excited the Class than any music that they heard during their journeys; and Master Beal made a record of it in verse, which we give at the close of the chapter.

The children of Germany learn to read music at the same age that

THE RHINEFELS.

they learn to read books. Music is a part of their primary school — Kindergarten — education. The poorest children are taught to sing.

The consequence is that the Germans are a nation of singers. The organ is a power in the church, the military band at the festival, and the ballad in the concert-room and the home.

These ballad-loving people are familiar with the best music. To them music is a language. Says Mayhew, in his elaborate work on the Rhine, in speaking of the free education in music in Germany: " To tickle the gustatory nerves with either dainty food or drink costs some money; but to be able to reproduce the harmonious combinations of a Beethoven or a Weber, or to make the air tremble melodiously with some sweet and simple ballad, or even to recall the sonorous solemnities of some prayerful chorus or fine thanksgiving in an oratorio, is not only to fill the heart and brain with affections too deep for words, but it is to be able to taste as high a pleasure as the soul is capable of knowing, and yet one that may be had positively for nothing."

It is to be regretted that so much of the good music of Germany is performed in the beer-gardens. The too free use of the glass and the pipe cannot tend to make the nation strong for the future; and one cannot long be charmed with the music and mirth of such places without fearing for the losses that may follow.

All trades and occupations have their own songs, even the humblest. Take for example the pleasing Miller's Song, which catches the spirit of his somewhat poetic yet homely calling: —

> "To wander is the miller's joy,
>   To wander!
> What kind of miller must he be,
> Who ne'er hath yearned to wander free?
>   To wander!
>
> "From water we have learned it, yes,
>   From water!
> It knows no rest by night or day,
> But wanders ever on its way,
>   Does water.
>
> "We see it by the mill-wheels, too,
>   The mill-wheels!
> They ne'er repose, nor brook delay,
> They weary not the livelong day,
>   The mill-wheels.
>
> "The stones, too, heavy though they be,
>   The stones, too,

>   Round in the giddy circle dance,
>   Ee'n fain more quickly would advance,
>   The stones would.
>
> "To wander, wander, my delight,
>   To wander!
> O master, mistress, on my way
> Let me in peace depart to-day,
>   And wander!"
>
> WILHELM MÜLLER.

The watchman, too, has his peculiar songs. One of these is very solemn and stately. A favorite translation of it begins: —

> "Hark ye, neighbors, and hear me tell
> *Eight* now strikes the loud church bell."

An almost literal translation thus reproduces the grand themes which were made to remind the old guardians of the night in their ghostly vigils : —

THE WATCHMAN'S SONG.

> Hark, while I sing! our village clock
> The hour of eight, good sirs, has struck.
> Eight souls alone from death were kept,
> When God the earth with deluge swept:
> Unless the Lord to guard us deign,
> Man wakes and watches all in vain.
>   Lord! through thine all-prevailing might,
>   Do thou vouchsafe us a good night!
>
> Hark, while I sing! our village clock
> The hour of nine, good sirs, has struck.
> Nine lepers cleansed returned not; —
> Be not thy blessings, man, forgot!
> Unless the Lord to guard us deign,
> Man wakes and watches all in vain.
>   Lord! through thine all-prevailing might,
>   Do thou vouchsafe us a good night!

Hark, while I sing! our village clock
The hour of ten, good sirs, has struck.
Ten precepts show God's holy will; —
Oh, may we prove obedient still!
Unless the Lord to guard us deign,
Man wakes and watches all in vain.
   Lord! through thine all-prevailing might,
   Do thou vouchsafe us a good night!

Hark, while I sing! our village clock
The hour eleven, good sirs, has struck.
Eleven apostles remained true; —
May we be like that faithful few!
Unless the Lord to guard us deign,
Man wakes and watches all in vain.
   Lord! through thine all-prevailing might,
   Do thou vouchsafe us a good night!

Hark, while I sing! our village clock
The hour of twelve, good sirs, has struck.
Twelve is of Time the boundary; —
Man, think upon eternity!
Unless the Lord to guard us deign
Man wakes and watches all in vain.
   Lord! through thine all-prevailing might,
   Do thou vouchsafe us a good night!

Hark, while I sing! our village clock
The hour of one, good sirs, has struck.
One God alone reigns over all;
Nought can without his will befall:
Unless the Lord to guard us deign,
Man wakes and watches all in vain.
   Lord! through thine all-prevailing might,
   Do thou vouchsafe us a good night!

Hark, while I sing! our village clock
The hour of two, good sirs, has struck.
Two ways to walk has man been given:
Teach me the right, — the path to heaven!
Unless the Lord to guard us deign,
Man wakes and watches all in vain.
   Lord! through thine all-prevailing might,
   Do thou vouchsafe us a good night!

Hark, while I sing! our village clock
The hour of three, good sirs, has struck.
Three Gods in one, exalted most,
The Father, Son, and Holy Ghost.
Unless the Lord to guard us deign,
Man wakes and watches all in vain.
   Lord! through thine all-prevailing might,
   Do thou vouchsafe us a good night!

Hark, while I sing! our village clock
The hour of four, good sirs, has struck.
Four seasons crown the farmer's care; —
Thy heart with equal toil prepare!
Up, up! awake, nor slumber on!
The morn approaches, night is gone!
   Thank God, who by his power and might
   Has watched and kept us through this night!

The Class devoted an autumn evening to singing the songs of the Rhine; the "Watch on the Rhine," the "Loreley," the student-songs, folk-songs, and some of the chorals of Luther. The song that proved most inspiring was the "Wild Chase of Lützow." Master Beal awakened a deep interest in this song before it was sung, by relating its history.

"THE WILD HUNT OF LÜTZOW."

All musical ears are familiar with the refrain: "Yes, 't is the hunt of Lützow the free and the bold," — if not with these exact words, with other words of the same meaning. The music of C. M. Von Weber has carried the "hunt" of Lützow over the world. The song and music alike catch the spirit and the movement of a corps of cavalry bent on the destruction of an enemy. One sees the flying horsemen in the poem, and hears them in the music. It was one of the few martial compositions that starts one to one's feet, and stirs one's blood with the memory of heroic achievements.

I will give you one of the most vigorous translations. Longfellow has adopted it in his "Poems of Places." It catches the spirit of the original, and very nearly reproduces the original thought.

LÜTZOW'S WILD CHASE.

What gleams from yon wood in the bright sunshine?
Hark! nearer and nearer 't is sounding;
It hurries along, black line upon line,
And the shrill-voiced horns in the wild chase join,
  The soul with dark horror confounding:
And if the black troopers' name you 'd know,
'T is Lützow's wild Jäger, — a-hunting they go!

MAYENCE IN THE OLDEN TIME.

From hill to hill, through the dark wood they hie,
  And warrior to warrior is calling;
Behind the thick bushes in ambush they lie,
The rifle is heard, and the loud war-cry,
  In rows the Frank minions are falling:

And if the black troopers' name you 'd know,
'T is Lützow's wild Jäger, — a-hunting they go!

Where the bright grapes glow, and the Rhine rolls wide,
  He weened they would follow him never;
But the pursuit came like the storm in its pride,
With sinewy arms they parted the tide,
  And reached the far shore of the river;
And if the dark swimmers' name you 'd know,
'T is Lützow's wild Jäger, — a-hunting they go!

How roars in the valley the angry fight;
  Hark! how the keen swords are clashing!
High-hearted Ritter are fighting the fight,
The spark of Freedom awakens bright,
  And in crimson flames it is flashing:
And if the dark Ritters' name you 'd know,
'T is Lützow's wild Jäger, — a-hunting they go!

Who gurgle in death, 'mid the groans of the foe,
  No more the bright sunlight seeing?
The writhings of death on their face they show,
But no terror the hearts of the freemen know.
  For the Franzmen are routed and fleeing;
And if the dark heroes' name you 'd know,
'T is Lützow's wild Jäger, — a-hunting they go!

The chase of the German, the chase of the free,
  In hounding the tyrant we strained it!
Ye friends, that love us, look up with glee!
The night is scattered, the dawn we see,
  Though we with our life-blood have gained it!
And from sire to son the tale shall go:
'T was Lützow's wild Jäger that routed the foe!

Lützow, the cavalry hero of Prussia, in the German war for freedom against the rule of Napoleon, was born in 1782. He was a famous hunter, and when Europe arose against Bonaparte in 1813, he called for volunteers of adventurous spirit for cavalry service: "hunters" of the enemy, who should hang about the French army, and, with the destructive vigilance of birds or beasts of prey, give the enemy no rest on the German side of the Rhine.

The boldest young men of Germany rushed to Lützow; noblemen, students, foresters. His corps of cavalry became the terror of the French army. The enemy could never tell where they would be found.

Among the young volunteers was Körner, the young German poet. He was a slender young man; but he had an heroic soul, and the cavalry corps of the fiery Lützow seemed to him the place for it. He joined the "wild hunters" in 1813.

"Germany rises," he said. "The Prussian eagle beats her wings; there is hope of freedom.

"I know what happiness can fruit for me in life; I know that the star of fortune shines upon me; but a mighty feeling and conviction animate me: no sacrifice can be too great for my country's freedom!"

The words glow.

He added, —

"I must forth, — I must oppose my breast to the storm. Can I celebrate the deeds of others in song, and not dare with them the danger?"

Körner's battle-songs became firebrands. He consecrated himself to his country in the village church near Zobten. He wrote the battle-hymn for the occasion, which was a service for the departing volunteers.

"We swore," he said, "the oath of fidelity to our cause. I fell upon my knees and implored God's blessing. The oath was repeated by all, and the officers swore it on their swords. Then Martin Luther's 'A Mighty Fortress is our God' concluded the ceremony."

He wrote a thrilling war-song on the morning of the battle of Danneberg, May 12, 1813. It ended with these words: —

> "Hark! hear ye the shouts and the thunders before ye?
> On, brothers, on, to death and to glory!
> We'll meet in another, a happier sphere!

On May 28, 1813, Major Von Lützow determined to set out on an expedition towards Thuringia, with his young cavalry and with Cossacks. Körner begged to accompany him. Lützow commissioned him as an officer. He was wounded, and left for a time helpless in a wood, on the 17th of June. In this condition he wrote his famous "Farewell to Life."

> "My deep wound burns," &c.

Körner recovered, but was suddenly killed in an engagement on August 26th.

THE SONGS OF THE RHINE. 265

The "Sword Song" of Körner which Von Weber's music has made famous, was written a few hours before his death. It was an inspiration to the German cause.

"Lützow's Wild Chase" thrilled Prussia. Like the "Watch on the Rhine" in the recent war, it was the word that fired the national pride, and nerved men to deeds that crowned the cause with glory.

"The Rhine! the Rhine!" shouted the young German heroes at last, looking down on the river.

"Is there a battle?" asked the officers, dashing on in the direction of the shout.

"No, the enemy has gone over the Rhine," was the answer. "The Rhine! the Rhine!"

Mr. Beal introduced a number of selections from German composers, the loved tone-poets, with interesting stories and anecdotes. We reproduce a part of these musical incidents, as they properly belong to the history of the river of song.

Taking up a selection from Schubert's famous symphony, he spoke feelingly of the author, and then gave some pictures of the lives of Beethoven and Bach.

THE AUTHOR OF THE ERL KING.

Poor Schubert! The composer of what operas, symphonies, overtures, choruses, masses, cantatas, sonatas, fantasias, arias! What tenderness was in his soul!—Listen to the "Last Greeting;" what fancy and emotion! listen to the "Fisher Maiden" and "Post Horn;" what refinement! listen to the "Serenade;" what devotion! hear the "Ave Maria"!

Dead at the age of thirty-one; dead after a life of neglect, leaving all these musical riches behind him!

Franz Schubert was born at Himmelpfortgrand, in 1797. His father was a musician, but a poor man. Franz was placed at the age of eleven among the choir-boys of the Court Chapel, where he remained five years, absorbed in musical studies, and making himself the master of the leading instruments of the orchestra.

To compose music was his life. His restless genius was ever at work; always seeking to produce something new, something better. The old masters, and especially Haydn, Mozart, and Beethoven, were his sources of study and inspiration. Music became his world, and all outside of it was strange and unexplored. All of his moods found expression in music: his love, his hopes, his wit, his sadness, and his dreams.

He seems to have composed his best works for the pure love of his art, with little thought of money or fame. Many of his best works he never heard performed. He left his manuscript scores scattered about his rooms, and so they were found in confusion after his decease.

A monument was erected to his memory. On it is the following simple but touching inscription: —

"The art of music buried here a rich possession, but yet far fairer hopes. Franz Schubert lies here. Born on the 30th of January, 1797, died on the 19th of November, 1828, thirty-one years old."

Fame almost failed to overtake him in life; his course was so rapid, and his works were so swiftly produced. It crowned his memory.

Schubert's magnificent symphony in C is one of the most beautiful works of the kind ever written, and lovers of orchestral music always delight to find it on the programme of an evening concert. It is a charm, an enchantment; it awakens feelings that are only active in the soul under exceptional influences. Yet the listener does not know to what he is listening: it is all a mystery; no one can tell what the composer intended to express by this symphony. We know that the theme is a noble one, — but what? that the soul of the writer must have been powerfully moved during its composition, — by what influences? It is an enigma: each listener may guess at the theme, and each will associate it with the subject most in harmony with his own taste.

In 1844 Robert Schumann, while looking over a heap of dusty manuscripts at Vienna, found this wonderful symphony, until then unknown. He was so much charmed with it that he sent it to Mendelssohn at Leipzig. It was there produced at the Gewandhaus concerts, won the admiration it deserved, and thence found its way to all the orchestras of the world. The youthfnl composer had been dead nearly twenty years when the discovery was made.

One of the best known of the dramatic German ballads is the Erl King.

The Erl King is Death. He rides through the night. He comes to a happy home, and carries away a child, galloping back to the mysterious land whence he came.

In this ballad a father is represented as riding with a dying child under his cloak. The Erl King pursues them.

Schubert gave the ballad its musical wings. I need not describe the music. It is on your piano. Let it tell the story.

BEETHOVEN'S BOYHOOD AT BONN.

Literary men have often produced their best works late in life. Longfellow cites some striking illustrations of this truth in *Morituri Salutamus:* —

> "It is too late ! Ah, nothing is too late
> Till the tired heart shall cease to palpitate.
> Cato learned Greek at eighty ; Sophocles
> Wrote his grand Œdipus, and Simonides
> Bore off the prize of verse from his compeers,
> When each had numbered more than fourscore years,
> And Theophrastus, at fourscore and ten,
> Had but begun his Characters of Men.
> Chaucer, at Woodstock with the nightingales,
> At sixty wrote the Canterbury Tales ;
> Goethe at Weimar, toiling to the last,
> Completed Faust when eighty years were past."

Such examples of late working are seldom found in musical art. Men seem to become musicians because of the inspiration born within them. This impelling force is very early developed.

Handel, the greatest musical composer of his own or any age, was so devoted to music in childhood that his father forbade his musical studies. At the age of eleven he as greatly delighted and surprised Frederic I. of Prussia by his inspirational playing; he was in youth appointed to a conspicuous position of organist in Halle.

Haydn surprised his friends by his musical talents at his *fifth* year. He had a voice of wonderful purity, sweetness, and compass, and was received as a choir-boy at St. Stephen's Church, Vienna.

Mozart's childhood is a household story. He was able to produce chords on the harpsichord at the age of three, and wrote music with correct harmonies at the age of six. Glück had made a musical reputation at the age of eighteen.

Mendelssohn was a brilliant pianist at six, and gave concerts at nine. Verdi was appointed musical director at Milan in youth. Rossini composed an opera at the age of sixteen, and ceased to compose music at forty.

No other art exhibits such remarkable developments of youthful genius; though many eminent poets like Pindar, Cowley, Pope, Mrs. Hemans, L. E. L., have written well in early youth. Music is a flower that blossoms early, and bears early fruit.

Music may justly be called the art of youth.

BEETHOVEN'S HOME AT BONN.

Beethoven was born at Bonn on the Rhine, 1770. He lived here twenty-two years. His musical character was formed here.

Beethoven was put at the harpsichord at the age of four years. He was able to play the most difficult music in every key at twelve years; and was appointed one of the court organists when fifteen.

The boy received this appointment, which was in the chapel of the Elector of Cologne, by the influence of Count Waldstein, who had discovered his genius. Here he was the organ prince.

The following curious anecdote is told of his skill at the organ: —

"On the last three days of the passion week the Lamentations of the Prophet Jeremiah were always chanted; these consisted of passages of from four to six lines, and they were sung in no particular time. In the middle of each sentence, agreeably to the old choral style, a *rest* was made upon one note, which rest the player on the piano (for the organ was not used on those three days) had to fill up with a voluntary flourish.

"Beethoven told Heller, a singer at the chapel who was boasting of his professional cleverness, that he would engage, that very day, to put him out, at such a place, without his being aware of it, so that he should not be able to proceed. He accepted the wager; and Beethoven, when he came to a passage that suited his purpose, led the singer, by an adroit modulation, out of the prevailing mode into one having no affinity with it, still, however, adhering to the tonic of the former key ; so that the singer, unable to find his way in this strange region was brought to a dead stand.

"Exasperated by the laughter of those around him, Heller complained to the elector, who (to use Beethoven's expression) 'gave him a most gracious reprimand, and bade him not play any more such clever tricks.'"

At Bonn young Beethoven devoted himself almost wholly to the organ. The memories of the Rhine filled his life, which ended so sadly on the Danube. Bonn and Beethoven are as one name to the English or American tourist.

THE FATHER OF ORGAN MUSIC.

Bach, the greatest organist and composer of organ music of the last century, was born at Eisenach, 1685, and had truly a remarkable history. His art was born in him. He wrote because he must write, and sung because he must sing.

His father was a court musician, and had a twin brother who occupied the same situation, and so much resembled him that their wives could not tell them apart. These twin brothers produced music nearly alike; their dispositions were identical ; when one was ill, the other was so likewise, and both died at the same time.

John Sebastian Bach was the brightest ornament of this music-loving family. His parents died in his boyhood, and his musical education was undertaken by his eldest brother, a distinguished organist. He fed on music as food.

An incident will show his spirit. He was eager to play more difficult music than his brother assigned. He noticed that his brother had a book of especially difficult pieces ; and he begged to be allowed to use it, but was denied. This book was kept locked in a cupboard, which had an opening just wide enough to admit the boy's thin hand. He was able to reach it, and, by rolling it in a certain way, to bring it out and replace it without unlocking the door. He began to copy it by moonlight, as no candle was allowed him in the evening, and in six months had reproduced in this manner the whole of the music. About this time his brother died, and the friendless lad engaged himself as a choir-singer, which gave him a temporary support.

Organ-music became a passion with him. He determined, at whatever sacrifice, to make himself the master of the instrument. He might go hungry, lose the delights of society; but the first organist in Germany he would be : nothing should be allowed to stand in the way of this purpose in life. He studied all masters. He made a long journey on foot to Lubeck to hear a great German master play the organ ; and when he heard him, he remained three months an unknown and secret auditor in the church.

A youth in which a single aim governs life early arrives at the harvest. Young manhood found Bach court organist in that Athens of Germany, Weimar. His fame grew until it reached the ears of Frederick the Great.

"Old Bach has come," joyfully said the King to his musicians, on learning that the great organist arrived in town.

He became blind in his last years, as did Handel. Ten days before his death his sight was suddenly restored, and he rejoiced at seeing the sunshine and the green earth again. A few hours after this strange occurrence, he was seized with an apoplectic fit. He died at the age of sixty-eight.

His organ-playing was held to be one of the marvels of Germany. He made the organ as it were a part of his own soul ; it expressed his thoughts like an interpreter, and swayed other hearts with the emotions of his own. His oratorios and cantatas were numbered by the hundred, many of which were produced only on a single occasion. His most enduring work is the Passion Music.

In 1850 a Bach Society was formed in London, and a revival of the works of the master followed. Bach wrote five passions, but only one for two choirs.

To the general audience much of the Passion music, as arranged for English choral societies, seems too difficult for appreciation ; but the over-choir at the beginning, the expression of suffering and darkness, and the so-called earthquake chorus, with its sudden and stupendous effects, impress even the uneducated ear.

The beauty and power of the oratorio as a work of art are felt in proportion to one's musical training ; but as a sublime tone-sermon, all may feel its force, and dream that the awful tragedy it represents is passing before them.

THE ORGAN-TEMPEST OF LUCERNE.

We came to fair Lucerne at even, —
How beauteous was the scene !
The snowy Alps like walls of heaven
Rose o'er the Alps of green :
The damask sky a roseate light
Flashed on the Lake, and low

A CITY OF THE RHINE.

Above Mt. Pilate's shadowy height
Night bent her silver bow.

We turnèd towards the faded fane,
How many centuries old !
And entered as the organ's strain
Along the arches rolled ;
Such as when guardian spirits bear
A soul to realms of light,
And melts in the immortal air
The anthem of their flight ;
Then followed strains so sweet,
So sadly sweet and low,
That they seemed like memory's music,
And the chords of long ago.

A light wind seemed to rise ;
A deep gust followed soon,
As when a dark cloud flies
Across the sun, at noon.
It filled the aisles, — each drew
His garments round his form ;
We could not feel the wind that blew,
We could only hear the storm.
Then we cast a curious eye
Towards the window's lights,
And saw the lake serenely lie
Beneath the crystal heights.
Fair rose the Alps of white
Above the Alps of green,
The slopes lay bright in the sun of night,
And the peaks in the sun unseen.

A deep sound shook the air,
As when the tempest breaks
Upon the peaks, while sunshine fair
Is dreaming in the lakes.
The birds shrieked on their wing ;
When rose a wind so drear,
Its troubled spirit seemed to bring
The shades of darkness near.
We looked towards the windows old,
Calm was the eve of June,
On the summits shone the twilight's gold,
And on Pilate shone the moon.

A sharp note's lightning flash
  Upturned the startled face;
When a mighty thunder-crash
  With horror filled the place!
From arch to arch the peal
  Was echoed loud and long;
Then o'er the pathway seèmed to steal
  Another seraph's song;
And 'mid the thunder's crash
  And the song's enraptured flow,
We still could hear, with charmèd ear,
  The organ playing low.

THE RIVER OF SONG.

As passed the thunder-peal,
  Came raindrops, falling near,
A rain one could not feel,
  A rain that smote the ear.
And we turned to look again
  Towards the mountain wall,
When a deep tone shook the fane,
  Like the avalanche's fall,
Loud piped the wind, fast poured the rain,
  The very earth seemed riven,
And wildly flashed, and yet again,
  The smiting fires of heaven.

And cheeks that wore the light of smiles
　　When slowly rose the gale,
Like pulseless statues lined the aisles
　　And, as forms of marble, pale.
The organ's undertones
　　Still sounded sweet and low,
And the calm of a more than mortal trust
　　With the rhythms seemed to flow.

The Master's mirrored face
　　Was lifted from the keys,
As if more holy was the place
　　As he touched the notes of peace.
Then the sympathetic reeds
　　His chastened spirit caught,
As the senses met the needs
　　And the touch of human thought.
The organ whispered sweet,
　　The organ whispered low,
"Fear not, God's love is with thee,
　　Though tempests round thee blow!"
And the soul's grand power 't was ours to trace,
　　And its deathless hopes discern,
As we gazed that night on the living face
　　Of the Organ of Lucerne.

Then from the church it passed,
　　That strange and ghostly storm,
And a parting beam the twilight cast
　　Through the windows, bright and warm.
The music grew more clear,
　　Our gladdened pulses swaying,
When Alpine horns we seemed to hear
　　On all the hillsides playing.

We left the church — how fair
　　Stole on the eve of June!
Cool Righi in the dusky air,
　　The low-descending moon!
No breath the lake cerulean stirred,
　　No cloud could eye discern;
The Alps were silent, — we had heard
　　The Organ of Lucerne.

Soon passed the night, — the high peaks shone
  A wall of glass and fire,
And Morning, from her summer zone,
  Illumined tower and spire ;
I walked beside the lake again,
  Along the Alpine meadows,
Then sought the old melodious fane
  Beneath the Righi's shadows.
The organ, spanned by arches quaint,
  Rose silent, cold, and bare,
Like the pulseless tomb of a vanished saint: —
  The Master was not there!
But the soul's grand power 't was mine to trace
  And its deathless hopes discern,
As I gazed that morn on the still, dead face
  Of the Organ of Lucerne.

CHAPTER XV.

COPENHAGEN.

COPENHAGEN. — THE STORY OF ANCIENT DENMARK. — THE ROYAL FAMILY. — STORY OF A KING WHO WAS PUT INTO A BAG.

N the Denmark Night Mr. Beal gave a short introductory talk on Copenhagen, and several of the boys related stories by Hans Christian Andersen. Master Lewis gave some account of the early history of Denmark and of the present Royal Family; and Herman Reed related an odd story of one of the early kings of Denmark.

"Copenhagen, or the Merchants' Haven, the capital of the island kingdom of Denmark, rises out of the coast of Zealand, and breaks the loneliness and monotony of a long coast line. It was a beautiful vision as we approached it in the summer evening hours of the high latitude, — evening only to us, for the sun was still high above the horizon. The spire of the Church of Our Saviour — three hundred feet high — appeared to stand against the sky. Palaces seemed to lift themselves above the sea as we steamed slowly towards the great historic city of the North.

"The entrance to the harbor is narrow but deep. The harbor itself is full of ships; Copenhagen is the station of the Danish navy.

"We passed very slowly through the water streets among the ships of the harbor, — for water streets they seemed, — and after a tedious landing, were driven through the crooked streets of a strange old town to a quiet hotel where some English friends we had met on the Continent were stopping.

"The city is little larger than Providence, Rhode Island. Its

THE PALACE OF ROSENBORG.

public buildings are superb. It is an intellectual city, and its libraries are the finest of Europe.

"It is divided into two parts, the old town and the new. In the new part are broad streets and fine squares.

"We visited the Rosenborg Palace, the old residence of the Danish kings;—it is only a show palace now. In the church we saw Thorwaldsen's statues of the Twelve Apostles, regarded as the finest of his works.

VIEW OF COPENHAGEN

THE STORY OF ANCIENT DENMARK.

It is a strange, wild romance, the early history of the nations of the North. The Greeks and Romans knew but little about the Scandinavians. They knew that there was a people in the regions from which came the north winds. The north wind was very cold. Was there a region beyond the north wind? If so, how lovely it must be, where the cold winds never blow. They fancied that there was such a region. They called the inhabitants Hyperboreans, or the people beyond the north wind. They imagined also that in this region of eternal summer men did not die. If one of the Hyperboreans became tired of earth, he had to kill himself by leaping from a cliff.

The Northmen, or the inhabitants of Denmark, Norway, and Sweden, were of the same origin as the tribes that peopled Germany, and that came from the East, probably from the borders of the Black Sea. They were fire-worshippers, and their chief god was Odin.

Denmark means *a land of dark woods*. In ancient times it was probably covered with sombre firs. One of its early kings was Dan the Famous. His descendants were called Danes.

Many ages after the reign of this king, the land was filled with peace and plenty. It was the Golden Age of the North. Frode the Peaceful was king in the Golden Age. He ruled over all lands from Russia to the Rhine, and over two hundred and twenty kingdoms of two hundred and twenty subjugated kings. There was no wrong, nor want, nor thieves, nor beggars in the Golden Age. This happy period of Northern history was at that age of the world when Christ was born.

According to the Scalds, the god Odin used to appear to men. He appeared the last time at the battle of Bravalla, a contest in which the Frisians, Wends, Finns, Lapps, Danes, Saxons, Jutes, Goths, and Swedes all were engaged. The dead were so thick on the field, after this battle, that their bodies reached to the axle-wheels of the chariots of the victors. At the time of this battle Christianity was being proclaimed in England. It was approaching the North. With the battle of Bravalla the mythic age of Denmark and the North comes to an end.

I have told you something of Louis le Debonnaire, who went to die on a rock in the Rhine, that the waters might lull him to his eternal repose. He was a missionary king, and he desired nothing so much as the conversion of the world to Christ. He was the son of Charlemagne. "It is nobler to convert souls than conquer kingdoms" was his declaration of purpose. He sent missionary apostles to the North to convert Denmark. His missions at first were failures, but in the end they resulted in giving all the Northern crowns to Christ's kingdom, that Louis loved more than his own.

The Danes in the Middle Ages became famous sea-kings. Before England, Denmark ruled the sea. One stormy day in December Gorm the Old appeared before Paris with seven hundred barks. He compelled the French king to sue for peace.

The sea-kings conquered England. Canute the Dane was king of all the regions of the northwest of Europe. His kingdom embraced Denmark, England, Sweden, Norway, Scotland, and Cumberland. Such is the second wonderful period of Denmark's history.

THE ROYAL FAMILY OF DENMARK.

Royal people, as well as "self-made men," often undergo remarkable changes of fortune. No one, however high or low, is free from the accidents of this world. All men have surprises, either good or bad, in store for them.

Few families have experienced a more striking change in position than the present royal house of the little northern kingdom of Denmark. Twenty years ago, the present king, Christian IX., was a rather poor and obscure gentleman, of princely rank, to be sure, residing quietly in Copenhagen, and bringing up his fine family of boys and girls in a very domestic and economical fashion. He was only a remote cousin of Frederick VII., the reigning monarch, and he seemed little likely to come to the throne.

But death somewhat suddenly prepared the way for him, so that when old Frederick died, in 1863, Christian found himself king.

This, however, was but the beginning of the fortunes of this once modest and little-known household. Just before Christian came to the throne, his eldest daughter, Alexandra, a beautiful and an amiable girl, attracted the attention of the Prince of Wales. The prince became attached to her, and in due time married her.

About the same time, Christian's second son, George, was chosen King of Greece, and was crowned at Athens, and is still reigning there.

After three years had passed, the second daughter, Maria Dagmar, who, like her sister Alexandra, was a very lovely and attractive girl, was married to the Czarowitch Alexander of Russia, after having been betrothed to his elder brother Nicholas, who died. She is now Empress of Russia.

PALACE OF FREIDERICKSBORG.

Somewhat later, the eldest son of the Danish king married the only daughter of Oscar II., King of Sweden and Norway, thus forming a new link of national friendship between the three Scandinavian nations.

It is thus quite possible that in the not distant future no less than four of King Christian's children, who were brought up with little more expectation than that of living respectably and wedding into Danish noble families, will occupy thrones in Europe. It may happen that the two daughters will share two of the greatest of those thrones,—that one will be Queen of England; the other is Empress of Russia,—while the two sons will be respectively King of Denmark and King of Greece.

This great good fortune, in a worldly point of view, which has come to the Danish royal family, cannot certainly be attributed solely, or even mainly, to luck or chance. It has been, after all, chiefly its virtues which have won it such a high position in Europe. The good breeding and excellent character of the king's children have won for them the prominence they now hold; for the daughters are as womanly and virtuous as they are physically attractive, and the sons are models of manly bearing and irreproachable habits.

THE STORY OF A KING WHO WAS PUT INTO A BAG.

"His realm was once a cradle, and now it is a coffin," might be said of the most powerful monarch that ever lived. Kings are but human, and they are pitiable objects indeed when they fall from their high estate into the power of their enemies. Never did a king present a more humiliating spectacle in his fall than Valdemar II., called the Conqueror.

Under the early reign of this king, the Golden Age seemed to have returned to Denmark. Never was a young monarch more prosperous or glorious in so narrow a kingdom.

His empire grew. He annexed Pomerania. He wrested from the German Empire all the territories in their possession north of the Elbe and Elde, and he finally became the master of Northern Germany.

He was a champion of the Church. A papal bull conceded to him the sovereignty of all the people he might convert, and he entered the field against pagans of Esthonia, with an army of 60,000 men, and 1,400 ships! He baptized the conquered with kingly pomp and pride.

His reign was now most splendid. Denmark was supreme in Scandinavia and Northern Germany. The Pope revered the Danish power, and the world feared it.

But secret foes are often more dangerous than open enemies. The conquered princes of Germany hated him, and planned his downfall.

Among these was the Count-Duke of Schwerin. He pretended great respect and affection for Valdemar. He laid many snares for the king's ruin, but they failed. He was called "Black Henry" in his own country on account of his dark

THE KING IN THE BAG.

face and evil nature, and Valdemar had been warned against him as a false friend.

But he was warm, obsequious, and fascinating to the king, and the king liked him.

In the spring of 1233 Valdemar invited him to hunt with him in the woods of Lyo.

"Tell the king I am disabled and cannot leave my couch," said the artful count, who now thought of a way to accomplish his long-cherished purpose.

He left his couch at once, and sent his spies to shadow the king.

The king landed at Lyo with only a few attendants.

One night the king was sleeping in the woods of Lyo in a rude, unguarded tent. His son was by his side.

They were awaked from slumber by an assault from unknown foes, and a sense of suffocation.

What had happened? The king could not move his arms; his head seemed enveloped in cloth. He could not see; his voice was stifled. He *felt* himself carried away.

Black Henry had entered the tent with his confidants, and had put the King of the North and his son into two bags, and tied them up, and was now hurrying away with them to the river.

Black Henry laid his two captives in the bottom of a boat like two logs, and hoisted sail; and Valdemar, whose kingdom was now only a bag, was blown away towards the German coast.

He was thrown into prison, and there lived in darkness and neglect. The Pope ordered his release, but it was not heeded. The Danes tried to rescue him, but were defeated.

He was at last set free on the agreement that he should pay a large ransom. He returned to his kingdom, but found his territory reduced to its old narrow limits. His glory was gone. His empire had been the North; it had also been a bag; and at last it was a coffin. Poor old man! His last years were peaceful, and in them he served Denmark well.

CHAPTER XVI.

NORWAY.

STOCKHOLM. — STORY OF THE HERO KING. — UPSALA. — NORWAY. — CHRISTIANIA. — KING OLAF. — DRONTHEIM. — THE FISHERMAN OF FAROE.

HE narrative of travel and history was continued by Mr. Beal.

"Strange is the evolution of cities.

"We are about to glance at Stockholm. Let us go back in imagination six hundred years.

"There are some rocky islands in the Baltic, at the foot of the northern peninsula. Sea birds wheel above them in the steel-gray air; they build their nests there. Storms sweep over these lonely islands; sunlight bursts upon them, and now and then a Viking's ship finds a haven among them, and scares away the birds.

"Years pass. Fishermen build huts on the islands. Hunters come there. There come also the sea kings. A mixed, strange people.

"They build a village on the holms, or islets. They defend themselves with stockades, and they found on stocks, or beams, their strong houses. The growing town rises from stock holms; hence, Stockholm.

"The years pass, and the sea birds fly away. There are wings of gables where once were wings of birds. Stockholm becomes a fortress, and, as in the case of St. Petersburg in recent times, the sea

GUSTAVUS ADOLPHUS.

desolation pulses with life and energy, and is transformed into a city. Churches, palaces, gardens, arise. Battles are fought, and here tread the feet of kings.

"The wonder grows. The birds scream far away now. The islands are spanned by bridges. Stockholm stands a splendid city, one of the crowns of earth.

"The city lies before us. Noble structures, villas, steeples, are seen among the green trees. The ships of many flags lie together like a town in the sea.

"It is sunset. The tops of the linden-trees are crowned with sunlight, the Gothic windows burn. A shadow falls from the gray sky. Afar fly the white sea-gulls. The shadow deepens. It is night. We are in Stockholm.

"Every nation has its hero.

"You have been told how that poor Louis le Debonnaire, the son of Charlemagne, preferred to win crowns for Christ's kingdom rather than for his own. He lost his own kingdom; but the missionaries he sent forth, though at first not successful, were the means of giving Christianity to all the nations of the North.

THE HERO KING OF SWEDEN.

There was born in Stockholm, in 1594, an heir to the Swedish throne, whose influence was destined to be felt throughout the world and to very distant periods of time. The child was named Gustavus Adolphus.

He was educated for the kingdom. At the age of ten he was made to attend the sittings of the Diet and the councils of state. In boyhood he was able to discuss state affairs in Latin, and in youth he was able to speak nearly all European tongues.

He was schooled in the arts of war as well as peace. In early manhood he entered Russia at the head of an army, and compelled the Czar to sue for peace.

After the war the young king gave his whole heart to the development of the industries and institutions of his kingdom. He founded schools, assisted churches, and everywhere multiplied influences for good. Never did a monarch devote himself more earnestly to the improvement of his people, or accomplish more in a short time. His influence for good has ever lived in Sweden, and is felt strongly to-day.

He was an ardent Protestant. The Catholic powers of the South and the Protestant powers of the North had become very hostile, and war between them seemed impending. In this crisis the Protestant leaders looked to Gustavus Adolphus as the champion of their cause.

In 1630 Gustavus called a Diet in Stockholm, and reported the danger that was threatening the Protestant states of Germany, and which would involve Sweden unless checked. He announced that he had decided to espouse the cause of the German princes, and to enter the field. He took his little daughter in his arms, and commended her to the Diet as the heir to the crown.

He landed in Germany on Midsummer's day in 1630. He had an army of fifteen thousand men. It was a small army indeed for so perilous an undertaking. "*Cum Deo et victricibus armis* is my motto," he declared, and trusting in this watchword he advanced on his dangerous course.

The Imperialists, as the foes of the Reformed Faith were called, were led by Wallenstein. They were greatly superior in numbers to the Swedes and their allies.

At Lutzen the great battle of Protestantism was fought, Nov. 6, 1632.

"I truly believe that the Lord has given my enemies into my hands," said Gustavus, just before the battle.

The morning dawned gray and gloomy. A heavy mist hung over the two armies.

The Swedish and German army united in singing Luther's hymn, —

"Ein' feste Burg ist unser Gott."

Then Gustavus said, —
"Let us sing 'Christ our Salvation.'"

> "Be not dismayed, thou little flock,
> Although the foe's fierce battle-shock,
> Loud on all sides, assail thee.
> Though o'er thy fall they laugh secure,
> Their triumph cannot long endure;
> Let not thy courage fail thee.
>
> "Thy cause is God's, — go at his call,
> And to his hand commit thy all;
> Fear thou no ill impending:

DEATH OF GUSTAVUS AND HIS PAGE.

His Gideon'shall arise for thee,
God's Word and people manfully,
In God's own time, defending.

"Our hope is sure in Jesus' might;
Against themselves the godless fight,
Themselves, not us, distressing;
Shame and contempt their lot shall be;
God is with us, with him are we:
To us belongs his blessing."

Clad in his overcoat without armor, he mounted his horse and rode along the lines.

"The enemy is within your reach," he said to the allies.

"Swedes," he said to his old army, "if you fight as I expect of you, you shall have your reward; if not, not a bone of your bodies will ever return to Sweden."

To the Germans he said, —

"If you fail me to-day, your religion, your freedom, and your welfare in this world and in the next are lost."

He prophesied to the Germans, —

"Trust in God; believe that with his help you may this day gain a victory which shall profit your latest descendants."

He waved his drawn sword over his head and advanced.

The Swedes and Finns responded with cheers and the clash of arms.

"Jesus, Jesus, let us fight this day for thy name," he exclaimed.

The whole army was now in motion, the king leading amid the darkness and gloom of the mist.

The battle opened with an immediate success for the Swedes. But in the moment of victory the king was wounded and fell from his horse.

"The king is killed!"

The report was like a death-knell to the Swedes, but only for a moment.

The king's horse with an empty saddle was seen galloping wildly down the road.

"Lead us again to the attack," the leaders demanded of George of Saxe-Weimar.

The spirit of the dead king seemed to infuse the little army with more than human valor. The men fought as though they were resolved to give their lives to their cause. The memory of the king's words in the morning thrilled them

Nothing could stand before such heroism. Pappenheim fell. The Imperialists were routed. The Swedes at night, victorious, possessed the field, but they had lost the bravest of kings, and one of the most unselfish of rulers.

"We left Stockholm for Upsala, the student city. The paddles of the boat brushed along the waters of the Mälar; the old city retreated from view, and landscape after landscape of variegated beauty rose before us.

"The Mälar Lake is margined with dark pines, bright meadows and fields, light green linden-trees, gray rocks, and shadowy woods. Here and there are red houses among the lindens.

"We pass flat-bottomed boats, that dance about in the current made by the steamer.

"The hills of Upsala come into view. The University next appears, like a palace; then a palace indeed, red like the houses; then the gabled town.

"We went to the church, and were conducted into a vaulted chamber where were crowns and sceptres taken from the coffins of dead kings. We wandered along the aisle after leaving the treasure-room of the dead, and gazed on cold tombs and dusty frescos.

"Here sleeps Gustavus Vasa.

"In the centre aisle, under a flat stone, lies the great botanist, Linnæus.

"We visited the garden of Linnæus, or the place where it once bore the blossoms and fruits of the world. Nettles were there; the orangeries were gone; the winter garden had disappeared. The place wore a desolate look; the master had departed, leaving little there but the ghost of a great memory.

"We left Stockholm for Norway.

"We were landed from the steamer at Christiansand. This seaport is a rude town, and except from the wild, strange expression of both land and sea, which affects one gloomily, yet with a kind of poetic

CASCADE IN NORWAY

sadness, revealed little to interest us or to remember. There was a
Lazaretto, or pest-house, on a high rock, from which we felt sure that
no disease would ever be communicated.

LAZARETTO.

"The scenery of Norway is unlike any other in the world. Take
the map and scan the western coast. It looks like a piece of lace-
work, so numerous are the inlets or fiords.

"These fiords are many of them surrounded by headlands as high
as mountain walls. They are little havens, with calm water of wondrous beauty and with walls that seem to reach to the sky. On a
level spot in the mountainous formation, a hamlet or a little church is
sometimes seen, one of the most picturesque objects with its setting
in the world."

[The artist can give one a better view of these fiords than any description, and he has faithfully done it here.]

THE NAERO FIORD.

"The mountains and valleys of Norway are unlike any other. Summer finds them as winter leaves them. Great hills are worn into cones by the snow and ice. The cataracts are numerous and wonderful. The water scenery has no equal for romantic beauty and wildness.

"A twelve hours' farther sail brought us to Christiania. It is situated in a lovely valley on the northern side of Christiania Fiord.

It has a population of about eighty thousand. Here are the Royal Palace and University.

"All of the cities of the North have great schools and libraries. The University at Christiania has nearly a thousand students, and a library of one hundred and fifty thousand books.

"The port is covered with ice during some four months in the year. During the mild seasons some two thousand vessels yearly enter the harbor.

"Olaf, the Saint, the King of 'Norroway,' who preached the Gospel 'with his sword,' is the hero of the western coast. I might relate many wonderful stories of him, but I would advise you to read 'The Saga of King Olaf,' by Longfellow, in the 'Wayside Inn.'

"His capital was Drontheim, far up among the northern regions, where the sun shines all night in summer, and where the winters are wild and dreary, cold and long. It is a quaint old town. Summer tourists to the western coast of Norway sometimes visit it. Its cathedral was founded by Olaf, and is nearly a thousand years old.

"And now in ten nights' entertainments, you have taken hasty views of Germany and the old Kingdom of Charlemagne. Narratives of travel and history have been mingled with strange traditions and tales of superstition; all have combined to give pictures of the ages that are faded and gone, and that civilization can never wish to recall. Men are reaching higher levels in religion, knowledge, science, and the arts. Kingcraft is giving way to the governing intelligence of the people, and superstition to the simple doctrines of the Sermon on the Mount and to the experiences of a spiritual life. The age of castles and fortresses, like churches, is gone. The age of peace and good-will comes with the fuller light of the Gospel and intelligence. The pomps of cathedrals will never be renewed. The Church is coming to teach that character is everything, and that the soul is the temple of God's spiritual indwelling."

The tenth evening was closed by Charlie Leland. He read an original poem, suggested by an incident related to him by a fisherman at Stockholm.

THE FISHERMAN OF FAROE.

When life was young, my white sail hung
  O'er ocean's crystal floor;
In the fiords alee was the dreaming sea,
  And the deep sea waves before.
The Faroe fishermen used to call
  From the pier's extremest post:
"Strike out, my boy, from the ocean wall;
  There's danger near the coast.
    Beware of the drifting dunes
    In the nights of the watery moons,
      Beware of the Maelstrom's tide
    When the western wind blows free,
    Of the rocks of the Skagerrack,
    Of the shoals of the Cattegat;
    Strike out for the open sea,
    Strike out for the open sea!"

"O pilot! pilot! every rock
  You know in the ocean wall."
"No, no, my boy, I only know
  Where there are no rocks at all,
Where there are no rocks at all, my boy,
  And there no ship is lost.
Strike out, strike out for the open sea;
  There's danger near the coast.
    Beware, I say, of the dunes
    In the nights of the watery moons,
      Beware of the Maelstrom's tide
    When the western wind blows free,
    Of the rocks of the Skagerrack,
    Of the shoals of the Cattegat;
    Strike out for the open sea,
    Strike out for the open sea!"

Low sunk the trees in the sun-laved seas,
  And the flash of peaking oars
Grew faint and dim on the sheeny rim
  Of the harbor-dented shores.

LAKE IN NORWAY.

And far Faroe in the light lay low,
Where rode like a dauntless host
The white-plumed waves o'er the green sea graves
Of the rock-imperilled coast.
And I thought of the drifting dunes
In the nights of the watery moons,
    And I thought of the Maelstrom's tide
When the western wind blew free,
Of the rocks of the Skagerrack,
Of the shoals of the Cattegat,
And I steered for the open sea,
I steered for the open sea.

To far Faroe I sailed away,
When bright the summer burned,
And I told in the old Norse kirk one day
The lesson my heart had learned.
Then the grizzly landvogt said to me:
"Of strength we may not boast;
But ever in life for you and me
There 's danger near the coast.
Then think of the drifting dunes
In the nights of the watery moons,
    And think of the Maelstrom's tide
When the western wind blows free,
Of the rocks of the Skagerrack,
Of the shoals of the Cattegat;
Strike out for the open sea,
Strike out for the open sea!"

"O landvogt, well thou knowest the ways
Wherein my feet may fall."
"Oh, no, my boy, I only know
The ways that are safe to all,
The ways that are safe to all, my boy,
And there no soul is lost.
Strike out in life for the open sea,
There 's danger near the coast.
Then think of the drifting dunes
In the nights of the watery moons,
    And think of the Maelstrom's tide
When the western wind blows free,
Of the rocks of the Skagerrack,
Of the shoals of the Cattegat;
Strike out for the open sea,
Strike out for the open sea!

"False lights, false lights, are near the land,
  The reef the land wave hides,
And the ship goes down in sight of the town
  That safe the deep sea rides.
'T is those who steer the old life near
  Temptation suffer most;
The way is plain to life's open main,
  There's danger near the coast.
    Beware of the drifting dunes
      In the nights of the watery moons,
        Beware of the Maelstrom's tide
      When the western wind blows free,
    Of the rocks of the Skagerrack,
    Of the shoals of the Cattegat;
      Strike out for the open sea,
      Strike out for the open sea!"

And so on life's sea I sailed away,
  Where free the waters flow,
As I sailed from the old home port that day
  For the islands of far Faroe.
And when I steer temptation near,
  The pilot, like a ghost,
On the wave-rocked pier I seem to hear:
  "There's danger near the coast.
    Beware of the drifting dunes
      In the nights of the watery moons,
        Beware of the Maelstrom's tide
      When the western wind blows free,
    Of the rocks of the Skagerrack,
    Of the shoals of the Cattegat;
      Strike out for the open sea,
      Strike out for the open sea!"

THE COAST.

CHAPTER XVII.

THE GREATER RHINE.

THE RETURN HOMEWARD. — ON THE TERRACE, — QUEBEC.

THE Class made their return voyage by the way of Liverpool to Quebec, one of the shortest of the ocean ferries, and one of the most delightful in midsummer and early autumn, when the Atlantic is usually calm, and the icebergs have melted away.

As the steamer was passing down the Mersey, and Liverpool with her thousands of ships, and Birkenhead with its airy cottages, were disappearing from view, Mr. Beal remarked to the boys. —

"We shall return through the Straits, and so shall be probably only four and a half days out of sight of land."

"I did not suppose it was possible to cross the Atlantic from land to land in four days and a half," said Charlie Leland.

"We shall stop to-morrow at Moville, the port of Londonderry," said Mr. Beal. "A few hours after we leave we shall sink the Irish coast. Make notes of the time you lose sight of the light-houses of Ireland, and of the time when you first see Labrador, and compare the dates towards the end of the voyage," said Mr. Beal.

Past the green hills of Ireland the steamer glided along, among ships so numerous that the sea seemed a moving city, or the suburbs of a moving city; for Liverpool itself, with her seven miles of wonderful docks, is a city of the sea.

The Giant's Causeway, the sunny port of Moville, the rocky islands with their white light-houses, were passed, and at one o'clock on Monday morning the last light dropped into the calm sea, fading like a star.

The Atlantic was perfectly calm — as "calm as a mill-pond" as the expression is, during the tranquillity of the ocean that follows the settled summer weather. The steamer was heavily loaded, and had little apparent motion; bright days and bright nights succeeded each other. A flock of gulls followed the steamer far out to sea. For three days no object of interest was seen on the level ocean except the occasional spouting of a whale.

The sky was a glory in the long twilights. The sun when half set made the distant ocean seem like an island of fire, and the light clouds after sunset like hazes drifting away from a Paradisic sphere.

On Thursday morning the shadowy coast of Labrador appeared. The voyage seemed now virtually ended after four days from land to land. There were three days more, but the steamer would be in calm water, with land constantly in view.

The Straits of Belle Isle, some six miles wide, were as calm as had been the ocean. The Gulf of St. Lawrence — the fishing field of the world — was like a surface of glass. The sunrise and moonrise were now magnificent; the sunsets brought scenes to view as wonderful as the skies of Italy; gigantic mountains rose; clustering sails broke the monotonous expanse of the glassy sea, and now and then appeared an Indian canoe such as Jacques Cartier and the early explorers saw nearly three centuries ago.

The wild shores of Anticosti rose and sunk.

"We are now in the Greater Rhine," said Mr. Beal to the boys, — "the Rhine of the West."

"How is that?" asked Charlie Leland. "Is not the Hudson the American Rhine?"

"It is the New York Rhine," said Mr. Beal, smiling. "The river

NIAGARA FALLS.

St. Lawrence is, by right of analogy, the American Rhine, and so deserves to be called."

"Which is the larger river?" asked Charlie.

"The larger?"

"Yes, the longer?"

"It does not seem possible that an American school-boy could seriously ask such a question! I am sometimes astonished, however, at the ignorance that older people of intelligence show in regard to our river of which all Americans should be proud.

"Ours is the Greater Rhine. The German Rhine is less than a thousand miles long; our Rhine is nearly twenty-five hundred miles long: the German Rhine can at almost any point be easily spanned with bridges; our Rhine defies bridges, except in its narrowest boundaries. The great inland seas of Superior, Huron, Michigan, Ontario, and Erie require a width of miles for their pathway to the ocean. The Rhine falls cannot be compared with Niagara, nor the scattered islands of the old river with the Lake of a Thousand Islands of the new. Quebec is as beautiful as Coblentz, and Montreal is in its situation one of the loveliest cities of the world.

"The tributaries of the old Rhine are small; those of the new are almost as large as the old Rhine itself,— the gloomy Saguenay, and the sparkling Ottawa.

"Think of its lakes! Lake Ladoga, the largest lake in Europe, contains only 6,330 square miles. Lake Superior has 32,000 square miles, and Michigan 22,000 square miles.

"You will soon have a view of the mountain scenery of the lower St. Lawrence. The pine-covered walls along which trail the clouds of the sky are almost continuous to Montreal."

"But why," asked Charlie Leland, "is the German Rhine so famous, and ours so little celebrated?"

"The German Rhine gathers around it the history of two thousand years; ours, two hundred years. What will our Rhine be two thousand years from to-day?"

He added: —

"I look upon New England as one of the best products of civilization thus far. But there is rising a new New England in the West, a vast empire in the States of the Northwest and in Canada, to which New England is as a province, — an empire that in one hundred years will lead the thought, the invention, and the statesmanship of the world. Every prairie schooner that goes that way is like a sail of the 'Mayflower.' ·

"In yonder steerage are a thousand emigrants. The easy-going, purse-proud cabin passengers do not know it; they do not visit them or give much thought to them: but there are the men and women whose children will one day sway the empire that will wear the crown of the world.

"The castles are fading from view on the hills of the old Rhine; towns and cities are leaping into life on the new. The procession of cities, like a triumphal march, will go on, on, on. The Canadian Empire will probably one day lock hands with the imperial States of the Northwest; Mexico, perhaps, will join the Confederacy, and Western America will doubtless vie with Eastern Russia in power, in progress, and in the glories of the achievements of the arts and sciences. Our Rhine has the future: let the old Rhine have the past."

The Class approached Quebec at night. The scene was beautiful: like a city glimmering against the sky, the lights of the lower town, of the upper town, and of the Castle standing on the heights, shone brightly against the hills; and the firing of guns and the striking of bells were echoed from the opposite hills of the calm and majestic river.

The Class spent a day at Quebec, chiefly on the Terrace, — one of the most beautiful promenades in the world. From the Terrace the boys saw the making up of the emigrant trains on the opposite side of the river, where the steamer had landed, and saw them disappear along the winding river, going to the great province of Ontario, the lone woods of Muskoka, and the far shores of the Georgian Bay.

A NEW ENGLAND IN THE WEST

NEAR QUEBEC.

"I wish we might make a Zigzag journey on the St. Lawrence," said Charlie Leland.

"And collect the old legends, stories, and histories of the Indian tribes, and the early explorers and French settlers," added Mr. Beal. "Perhaps some day we may be able to do so. I am in haste to return to the States, but I regret to leave a place so perfectly beautiful as the Terrace of Quebec. It is delightful to sit here and see the steamers go and come; to watch the bright, happy faces pass, and to recall the fact that the river below is doubtless to be the water-path of the nations that will most greatly influence future times. But our journey is ended: let us go."

ON THE TERRACE,—QUEBEC.

Alone, beside these peaceful guns
  I walk,— the eye is calm and fair;
Below, the broad St. Lawrence runs,
  Above, the castle shines in air,
And o'er the breathless sea and land
Night stretches forth her jewelled hand.

Amid the crowds that hurry past—
  Bright faces like a sunlit tide —
Some eyes the gifts of friendship cast
  Upon me, as I walk aside,
Kind, wordless welcomes understood,
The Spirit's touch of brotherhood.

Below, the sea; above, the sky,
  Smile each to each, a vision fair;
So like Faith's zones of light on high,
  A sphere seraphic seems the air,
And loving thoughts there seem to meet,
And come and go with golden feet.

Below me lies the old French town,
  With narrow rues and churches quaint,
And tilèd roofs and gables brown,
  And signs with names of many a saint.
And there in all I see appears
The heart of twice an hundred years.

Beyond, by inky steamers mailed,
  Point Levi's painted roofs arise,
Where emigration long has hailed
  The empires of the western skies;
And lightly wave the red flags there,
Like roses of the damask air.

Peace o'er yon garden spreads her palm,
  Where heroes fought in other days;
And Honor speaks of brave Montcalm
  On Wolfe's immortal shaft of praise.
What lessons that I used to learn
In schoolboy days to me return!

Fair terrace of the Western Rhine,
  I leave thee with unwilling feet,
I long shall see thy castle shine
  As bright as now, in memories sweet;
And cheerful thank the kindly eyes
That lent to me their sympathies.

Go, friendly hearts, that met by chance
  A stranger for a little while;
Friendship itself is but a glance,
  And love is but a passing smile.
I am a pilgrim, — all I meet
Are glancing eyes and hurrying feet.

Farewell; in dreams I see again
  The northern river of the vine,
While crowns the sun with golden grain
  The hillsides of the greater Rhine.
And here shall grow as years increase
The empires of the Rhine of Peace.

CELEBRATED WAR STORIES.

THE BOYS OF '61.
OR FOUR YEARS OF FIGHTING. A record of personal observation with the Army and Navy from the battle of Bull Run to the fall of Richmond. By CHARLES CARLETON COFFIN, author of "The Boys of '76," "Our New Way 'Round the World," "The Story of Liberty," "Winning His Way," "Old Times in the Colonies," etc. With numerous illustrations.
1 vol., 8vo, chromo-lithographed board covers and linings $1.75
1 vol., 8vo, cloth, gilt 2.50

THE SAILOR BOYS OF '61.
By Prof. J. RUSSELL SOLEY, author of "The Boys of 1812," etc. This volume contains an accurate and vivid account of the naval engagements of the great Civil War, and the deeds of its heroes. Elaborately and beautifully illustrated from original drawings.
1 vol., 8vo, chromo-lithographed board covers, ... $1.75
1 vol., 8vo, cloth gilt, . . 2.50

THE BOYS OF 1812.
By Prof. J. RUSSELL SOLEY, author of "Blockaders and Cruisers," "The Sailor Boys of '61," etc., etc. This "most successful war book for the young, issued last year," is now made boards with an illustrated cover designed by Barnes.
1 vol., 8vo, chromo-lithographed board covers $1.75
1 vol., 8vo, cloth gilt, . . 2.50

"Prof. SOLEY's books should be read by every American boy, who cares for the honor of his country." — *Boston Beacon.*

"He must be a dull boy who can read such records of heroism without a quickening of the pulses." — *San Francisco Chronicle.*

"We are in no danger of cultivating too much patriotism, and such a book as this is an excellent educator along an excellent line of thought." — *Chicago Daily Inter-Ocean.*

The Sixth Mass. Regiment passing through Baltimore.

MY DAYS AND NIGHTS ON THE BATTLEFIELD.
By CHARLES CARLETON COFFIN. With eighteen full-page plates. Small quarto. Bound in illuminated board covers. $1.25

FOLLOWING THE FLAG.
By CHARLES CARLETON COFFIN. With eighteen full-page plates. Small quarto. Bound in illuminated board covers, ... $1.25

WINNING HIS WAY.
By CHARLES CARLETON COFFIN. With twenty-one full-page plates Small quarto. Bound in illuminated board covers, ... $1.25

THE CARLETON SERIES OF JUVENILES,
CONSISTING OF
WINNING HIS WAY, FOLLOWING THE FLAG.
MY DAYS AND NIGHTS ON THE BATTLEFIELD.
3 vols., 16mo, cloth, in a box, ... $3.75
Any volume sold separately, ... 1.25

ESTES & LAURIAT, Publishers, BOSTON, MASS.

THE FOUR GREAT ANNUALS.

CHATTERBOX FOR 1891.

This name, a household word in every home in the land, has become endeared in the hearts of two generations, and the readers of the early volumes are now men and women, who know that no books will delight their children more, or instruct them to a greater extent, than these dear old annual volumes, whose sales have long since mounted above the million mark.

This authorized reprint from duplicates of the original English plates, contains a large amount of copyright American matter, which cannot be reprinted by any other firm.

The Genuine Chatterbox contains a great variety of original stories, sketches and poems for the young, and every illustration which appears in it is expressly designed for this work, by the most eminent English artists. It has over 200 full-page original illustrations.

This year, to add to the enormous sales, no expense or trouble have been spared in securing a paper that would do entire justice to this royal juvenile, and make the illustrations appear to their best advantage, and if possible, bring the book nearer the zenith of juvenile perfection.

1 vol., quarto, illuminated board covers, ... $1.25
1 vol., quarto, cloth, black and gold stamps, ... 1.75
1 vol., quarto, cloth, extra, chromo, gilt side and edges, ... 2.25

LITTLE ONES ANNUAL.

Illustrated Stories and Poems for the Little Ones Edited by WILLIAM T. ADAMS (Oliver Optic). This beautiful volume consists of original stories and poems by the very best writers of juvenile literature, carefully selected and edited. It is embellished with 370 entirely original illustrations, drawn expressly for the work by the most celebrated book illustrators in America, and engraved on wood in the highest style, under the superintendence of George T. Andrew.

1 vol., quarto, illuminated board covers, . ' $1.75
1 vol., quarto, cloth and gilt, . . 2.25

"Little Ones Annual is by all odds the best thing of the season for children from five to ten years old."— *Boston Journal.*

THE NURSERY—T.

For 26 years the Nursery has been welcomed in thousands of families as the favorite picture book for our little folks, and the best of it is it improves in quality every year. It is now enlarged in size and crowded with charming stories and original artistic illustrations. Edited by OLIVER OPTIC

1 vol., royal octavo, illuminated covers, ... $1.25

OLIVER OPTIC'S ANNUAL, 1891.

A volume edited by OLIVER OPTIC appeals at once to the heart of every boy and girl, with all of whom his name is a synonym for everything bright and entertaining in juvenile literature.

This is the leading book of its kind of the year, with original illustrations.

1 vol., quarto, illuminated board covers and frontispiece, ... $1.50

ESTES & LAURIAT, Publishers, BOSTON, MASS

ENTERTAINING JUVENILES.

SCHOOLBOYS OF ROOKESBURY;
Or, The Boys of the Fourth Form. An entertaining story of the mishaps and adventures of several boys during a term at an English school. Edited by LAWRENCE H. FRANCIS. Fully illustrated with original drawings.
1 vol., small quarto, illuminated board cover $1.25

QUEEN HILDEGARDE ;
By LAURA E. RICHARDS, author of "Four Feet, Two Feet, and No Feet " A new edition of this popular girl's book, — a second " Little Women," — containing nineteen illustrations from new and original drawings.
1 vol., small quarto, illuminated board covers $1.50
" We should like to see the sensible, heroine loving girl in her early teens who would not like this book. Not to like it would simply argue a screw loose somewhere." — BOSTON POST.

THE DAYS OF CHIVALRY;
Or, Page, Squire and Knight. A highly interesting and instructive, historical romance of the Middle Ages. Edited by W. H. Davenport Adams, author of " Success in Life," " The Land of the Incas," etc. Thoroughly illustrated with 113 drawings.
1 vol., small quarto, illuminated board covers $1.50

THE RED MOUNTAIN OF ALASKA.
By WILLIS BOYD ALLEN. An exciting narrative of a trip through this most interesting but little known country, with accurate description of the same. Full of adventures, vividly portrayed by choice, original illustrations, by F. T. Merrill and others.
1 vol., 8vo, cloth, gilt, ... $2.50
" It throws ' Robinson Crusoe ', the ' Swiss Family Robinson', and all those fascinating phantasies, hopelessly into the shade, and will hold many a boy spellbound, through many an evening, of many a winter." — CHICAGO TRIBUNE.

HUNTING IN THE JUNGLE
WITH GUN AND GUIDE. From Les Animaux Sauvages, by WARREN F. KELLOGG. An exciting and amusing series of adventures in search of large game — gorillas, elephants, tigers and lions — fully illustrated with over a hundred original drawings by celebrated artists, engraved on wood by the best modern book illustrators.
1 vol., 8vo, chromo-lithographed board covers $1.75
1 vol., 8vo, cloth, gilt, ... 2.50

OUR NEW WAY 'ROUND THE WORLD.
By CHARLES CARLETON COFFIN, author of "The Story of Liberty," "The Boys of '61," "Following the Flag," "The Boys of '76," "Winning His Way," "My Days and Nights on the Battlefield," etc., etc. A new REVISED edition of this standard book of travel, which is interesting and useful to young and old; with a large number of additional illustrations.
1 vol., 8vo, chromo-lithographed board covers, ... $1.75
1 vol., 8vo, cloth, gilt, ... 2.50

TRAVELS IN MEXICO.
By F. A. OBER. A brilliant record of a remarkable journey from Yucatan to the Rio Grande Historic ruins, tropic wilds, silver hills are described with eloquence. No country possesses so rich a field for the historian, antiquarian, fortune-hunter, and traveller.
1 vol., 8vo, chromo-lithographed board covers $1.75
1 vol., 8vo, cloth, gilt, . . . 2.50

DICKENS'S CHILD'S HISTORY OF ENGLAND.
Holiday edition, with 100 fine illustrations, by De Neuville, Emile Bayard, F. Lix, and others.
1 vol., 8vo chromo-lithographed board covers $1.75
1 vol., 8vo, cloth, gilt, ... 2.50

THE YOUNG MOOSE HUNTERS.
By C. A. STEPHENS, author of the " Knockabout Club in the Tropics," etc., etc. With numerous full-page original illustrations made expressly for this edition. An exciting account of a hunting trip through the Maine woods.
1 vol., small quarto, illuminated board covers $1.50

SIX GIRLS.
By FANNY BELLE IRVING. A charming story of every-day home life, pure in sentiment and healthy in tone. A beautiful book for girls. Fully illustrated from original designs.
1 vol., small quarto, illuminated board covers and linings, ... $1.50

HANS CHRISTIAN ANDERSEN'S FAIRY TALES.
The standard authorized edition. A new translation from the original Danish edition, complete and unabridged, fully illustrated with engravings made from the original drawings, with an appropriate cover designed by L. S. IPSEN.
1 vol., quarto, cloth, $2.25

FEATHERS, FURS AND FINS;
OR STORIES OF ANIMAL LIFE FOR CHILDREN. A collection of the most fascinating stories about birds, fishes and animals, both wild and domestic, with illustrations drawn by the best artists, and engraved in the finest possible style by Andrew.
1 vol., quarto, chromo-lithographed board covers, . . . $1.75
1 vol., quarto, cloth and gilt, . . . 2.50

ESTES & LAURIAT, Publishers, BOSTON, MASS.

THE FAMOUS ZIGZAG SERIES.

The Most Entertaining and Instructive, the Most Successful and Universally Popular Series of Books for the Young Ever Issued in America.

Over Three Hundred Thousand Volumes of the Series have already been sold in this Country alone.

Zigzag Journeys in Australia;
Or, a Visit to the Ocean World. Describing the wonderful resources and natural advantages of the fifth continent, giving an insight into the social relations of the people and containing stories of gold discoveries and of the animals peculiar to this fascinating country.

1 vol., small quarto, illuminated board covers and linings, - - - - - - - - - - $1.75
1 vol., small quarto, cloth, bevelled and gilt, - 2.25

Uniform in style and price with the above, the other volumes of the series can be had as follows:

Zigzag Journeys in the Great North-West;
Or, a Trip to the American Switzerland. Giving an account of the marvelous growth of our Western Empire, with legendary tales of the early explorers. Full of interesting, instructive and entertaining stories of the New Northwest, the country of the future.

Zigzag Journeys in the British Isles.
With excursions among the lakes of Ireland and the hills of Scotland. Replete with legend and romance. Over 100 illustrations.

Zigzag Journeys in the Antipodes.
This volume takes the reader to Siam, and with delightful illustration and anecdote, tells him of the interesting animal worship of the country. Ninety-six illustrations.

Zigzag Journeys in India;
Or, the Antipodes of the Far East. A collection of Zenānā Tales. With nearly 100 fine original illustrations.

Zigzag Journeys in the Sunny South.
In which the Zigzag Club visits the Southern States and the Isthmus of Panama. With romantic stories of early voyagers and discoverers of the American continent. Seventy-two illustrations.

Zigzag Journeys in the Levant.
An account of a tour of the Zigzag Club through Egypt and the Holy Land, including a trip up the Nile, and visit to the ruins of Thebes, Memphis, etc. 114 illustrations.

Zigzag Journeys in Acadia & New France.
In which the Zigzag Club visits Nova Scotia and Acadia — "the Land of Evangeline," — New Brunswick, Canada, the St. Lawrence, Montreal, Quebec, etc., with romantic stories and traditions connected with the early history of the country. 102 illustrations.

Zigzag Journeys in Northern Lands.
From the Rhine to the Arctic Circle. Zigzag Club in Holland, Belgium, Germany, Denmark, Norway, and Sweden, with picturesque views, entertaining stories, etc. 119 illustrations.

Zigzag Journeys in the Occident.
A trip of the Zigzag Club from Boston to the Golden Gate; including visits to the wheat-fields of Dakota, the wonders of the Yellowstone and Yosemite. 148 illustrations.

Zigzag Journeys in the Orient.
A journey of the Zigzag Club from Vienna to the Golden Horn, the Euxine, Moscow, and St. Petersburg; containing a description of the Great Fair at Nijni-Novgorod, etc. 147 illustrations.

Zigzag Journeys in Classic Lands;
Or, Tommy Toby's Trip to Parnassus. An account of a tour of the Zigzag Club in France, Italy, Greece, Spain and Portugal. 124 illustrations.

Zigzag Journeys in Europe;
Or, Vacation Rambles in Historic Lands. In which the Zigzag Club travels through England, Scotland, Belgium, and France; with interesting stories and legends. 126 illustrations.

ESTES & LAURIAT, Publishers, BOSTON, MASS.

THE FAMOUS VASSAR GIRL SERIES.

☞ "Mrs. Champney's fame as the authoress of the delightful series of travels by the 'Three Vassar Girls,' has extended throughout the English-speaking world."

Three Vassar Girls in the Tyrol.
An entertaining description of the travels of our Vassar friends through this well-known country, giving an interesting account of the Passion Play at Ober Ammergau. Illustrated by "Champ" and others.
1 vol., small quarto, illuminated board covers and linings, - - - - - - - - $1.50
1 vol., small quarto, cloth, bevelled and gilt, - 2.00

Uniform in style and price with the above, the other volumes of the series can be had as follows:

Three Vassar Girls in Switzerland.
By ELIZABETH W. CHAMPNEY. An exceedingly interesting story interwoven with bits of Swiss life, historic incidents, and accounts of happenings at Geneva, Lucerne, and the Great St. Bernard. Illustrated by "Champ" and others.

Three Vassar Girls in Russia and Turkey.
During the exciting scenes and events of the late Turko-Russian war, with many adventures, both serious and comic. Profusely illustrated from original designs, by "CHAMP" and others.

Three Vassar Girls in France.
A story of the siege of Paris. A thrilling account of adventures when Germany and France were engaged in their terrible struggle. Ninety-seven illustrations by "CHAMP," DETAILLE, and DE NEUVILLE.

Three Vassar Girls at Home.
Travels through some of our own States and Territories, with many interesting adventures. Ninety-seven illustrations by "CHAMP."

Three Vassar Girls on the Rhine.
Full of amusing incidents of the voyage and historic stories of the castles and towns along the route. 128 illustrations by "CHAMP" and others.

Three Vassar Girls in Italy.
Travels through the vineyards of Italy, visiting all the large cities, and passing some time in Rome, in the Vatican, the Catacombs, etc. 107 illustrations.

Three Vassar Girls in South America.
A trip through the heart of South America, up the Amazon, across the Andes, and along the Pacific coast to Panama. 112 illustrations.

Three Vassar Girls in England.
Sunny memories of a holiday excursion of three college girls in the mother country, with visits to historic scenes and notable places. Ninety-eight illustrations.

Three Vassar Girls Abroad.
The vacation rambles of three college girls on a European trip for amusement and instruction, with their haps and mishaps. Ninety-two illustrations.

THE NEW SERIES.

Great Grandmother's Girls in New Mexico.
By ELIZABETH W. CHAMPNEY. This is the second volume of this delightful series describing incidents in the life of a quaint little maiden who lived in the time of the Spanish adventurers. Illustrated by "CHAMP."
1 vol., 8vo, chromo-lithographed board covers $1.75
1 vol., 8vo, cloth, gilt - - - - - - 2.50

Great Grandmother's Girls in France.
By ELIZABETH W. CHAMPNEY. A charming volume for girls, consisting of romantic stories of the heroines in the early colonial days—their privations and courage.
1 vol., 8vo, chromo-lithographed board covers $1.75
1 vol., 8vo, cloth, gilt, - - - - - 2.50

"A beautiful volume and one that cannot fail to arouse intense interest."—*Toledo Blade.*

"An excellent present for a boy or girl."—*Boston Transcript.*

ESTES & LAURIAT, Publishers, BOSTON, MASS.

THE FAMOUS "KNOCKABOUT CLUB" SERIES.

"Delightful and wholesome books of stirring out-door adventure for healthy American boys; books whose steadily increasing popularity is but a well-earned recognition of intrinsic merit."

THE KNOCKABOUT CLUB ON THE SPANISH MAIN.
By FRED A. OBER. In which the Knockabout Club visits Caracas, La Guayra, Lake Maracaibo, etc. Containing stories of the exploits of the pirates of the Spanish Main. Fully illustrated.
1 vol., small quarto, illuminated board covers and linings, - - - - $1.50
1 vol., small quarto, cloth, bevelled and gilt, - - - - - $2.00

Uniform in style and price with the above, the other volumes of the series can be had as follows:

THE KNOCKABOUT CLUB IN NORTH AFRICA.
By FRED A. OBER. An account of a trip along the coast of the Dark Continent, caravan journeys, and a visit to a pirate city, with stories of lion hunting and life among the Moors. Fully illustrated.

THE KNOCKABOUT CLUB IN SPAIN.
By FRED A. OBER. A panorama of Seville, the Guadalquivir, the Palaces of the Moors, the Alhambra, Madrid, Bull-fights, etc. Full of original illustrations, many full-page.

THE KNOCKABOUT CLUB IN THE ANTILLES.
By FRED A. OBER. A visit to the delightful islands that extend in a graceful line from Florida to South America, accompanied by a "Special Artist." 78 illustrations.

THE KNOCKABOUT CLUB IN THE EVERGLADES.
By FRED A. OBER. A visit to Florida for the purpose ef exploring Lake Okechobee, on which trip the boys encounter various obstacles and adventures with alligators, etc. 55 illustrations.

THE KNOCKABOUT CLUB IN THE TROPICS.
By C. A. STEPHENS. From the ice-fields of the North to the plains of New Mexico, thence through the "Land of the Aztecs," and the wonderful ruins of Central America, to the "Queen of the Antilles." 105 illustrations.

THE KNOCKABOUT CLUB ALONGSHORE.
By C. A. STEPHENS. A journey alongshore from Boston to Greenland, with descriptions of seal-fishing, Arctic Scenery, and stories of the ancient Northmen. 137 illustrations.

THE KNOCKABOUT CLUB IN THE WOODS.
By C. A. STEPHENS. A boy's book of anecdotes and adventures in the wilds of Maine and Canada. An account of a vacation spent in healthy amusement, fascinating adventure, and instructive entertainment. 117 illustrations.

ESTES & LAURIAT, Publishers, BOSTON, MASS.

YOUNG FOLKS' HISTORIES

YOUNG FOLKS' HISTORY OF THE NETHERLANDS.
A concise history of Holland and Belgium, from the earliest times, in which the author goes over the ground covered by Motley in his standard histories of these most interesting countries, and brings the narrative down to the present time. By ALEXANDER YOUNG. 150 illustrations.

YOUNG FOLKS' HISTORY OF AMERICA.
From the earliest times to the present. A new edition. With a chapter and additional illustrations on the Life and Death of President Garfield. Edited by H. BUTTERWORTH, author of "Zigzag Journeys." With 157 illustrations. Over 10,000 copies sold in one year.

YOUNG FOLKS' HISTORY OF MEXICO.
Comprising the principle events from the sixth century to the present time By FRED. A. OBER, author of "Camps in the Caribbees." With 100 illustrations.
The intimate relations of our country with Mexico, which the railroads and mines are developing, make this volume one of the most important in the entire series.

YOUNG FOLKS' HISTORY OF RUSSIA.
By NATHAN HASKELL DOLE. With 110 illustrations.

THE GREAT CITIES OF THE WORLD.

YOUNG FOLKS' HISTORY OF LONDON.
With graphic stories of its historic landmarks. By W. H. RIDEING. With 100 illustrations.

YOUNG FOLKS' HISTORY OF BOSTON.
By H. BUTTERWORTH, author of "Zigzag Journeys," etc. With 140 illustrations.

CHARLOTTE M. YONGE. YOUNG FOLKS' HISTORIES.

YOUNG FOLKS' BIBLE HISTORY. With 132 illustrations.
YOUNG FOLKS' HISTORY OF ENGLAND. With 60 illustrations by De Neuville, E. Bayard and others.
YOUNG FOLKS' HISTORY OF FRANCE. With 84 illustrations by A. De Neuville, E. Bayard and others.
YOUNG FOLKS' HISTORY OF ROME. With 114 illustrations.
YOUNG FOLKS' HISTORY OF GREECE. With 51 illustrations.
YOUNG FOLKS' HISTORY OF GERMANY. With 82 illustrations.

YOUNG FOLKS' EPOCHS OF HISTORY.

YOUNG FOLKS' HISTORY OF THE CIVIL WAR.
A concise and impartial account of the late war, for young people, from the best authorities both North and South. By MRS. C. EMMA CHENEY. Illustrated with 100 engravings, maps and plans.

YOUNG FOLKS' HISTORY OF THE REFORMATION.
IN GERMANY, FRANCE, ENGLAND AND OTHER COUNTRIES By FRED H. ALLEN. A graphic account of the men and the movements by which the great religious revolution which resulted in the establishment of Protestantism was carried on, from the early centuries of Christianity to the end of the Reformation. Fully illustrated.

YOUNG FOLKS' HISTORY OF THE QUEENS OF SCOTLAND.
These valuable books are condensed from Strickland's Queens of Scotland by ROSALIE KAUFMAN, and are at once reliable and entertaining to both old and young folks. Fully illustrated. 2 vols., 16mo, cloth.   .   . $3.00.

YOUNG FOLKS' HISTORY OF THE QUEENS OF ENGLAND.
From the Norman Conquest. Founded on Strickland's Queens of England. Abridged, adapted and continued to the present time. By ROSALIE KAUFMAN. With nearly 300 illustrations. 3 vols., 16mo, cloth   . $4.50.

LIBRARY OF ENTERTAINING HISTORY.
Edited by Arthur Gilman, M. A.

INDIA.   By FANNIE ROPER FEUDGE. With 100 illustrations, .   .   . $1.50
EGYPT.   By Mrs. CLARA ERSKINE CLEMENT. With 108 illustrations,   .   .   1.50
SPAIN.   By Prof. JAMES HERBERT HARRISON. With 111 illustrations,   .   .   1.50
SWITZERLAND.   By Miss HARRIET D. S. MACKENZIE. With 100 illustrations,   .   1.50
HISTORY OF AMERICAN PEOPLE. With 175 illustrations,   .   .   1.50

All the above volumes are published as 16mos, in cloth, at $1.50.

ESTES & LAURIAT, PUBLISHERS.
BOSTON, MASS.

HOUSEHOLD NECESSITIES.

SOCIAL CUSTOMS.

New edition, REDUCED IN PRICE. Complete Manual of American Etiquette. By FLORENCE HOWE HALL, daughter of Mrs. Julia Ward Howe. Handsomely printed, and neatly bound in extra cloth, gilt top, uncut. Small 8vo. - - - - - - - - $1.75

DO YOU ALWAYS KNOW JUST WHAT TO DO? Do you know how to encourage Mrs. D. Lightful, accept and return her courtesies, as they deserve; and politely but firmly avoid and defeat Mrs. Bore in her inroads on your privacy and more agreeable engagements? If you do not, let us recommend for EVERY SOCIAL QUESTION the above entertaining and instructive book, or its new baby relative, "THE CORRECT THING," mentioned below, for with these two books, one can make no mistake in life, as every possible question may be answered from their combined wisdom. They are *comprehensive, practical, reliable and authoritative.*

THE CORRECT THING.

By FLORENCE HOWE HALL, author of "Social Customs." 18mo. Very neatly bound in extra cloth, gilt top, - - - - - - - - - - - - - $0.75
Same, Bound in full flexible morocco, gilt edges (in a box). - - - - $1.25

This new manual is neatly printed in a size not too large to be slipped into the pocket, and is arranged so that one page reminds the reader that " IT IS THE CORRECT THING " to do this, while *per contra* the opposite page tells him that " IT IS NOT THE CORRECT THING " to do that. Its conciseness recommends it to many who would not take the time to master any more comprehensive manual.

"It is, indeed, a treasure of good counsel, and, like most advice, it has the merit of not being expensive."—*Montreal Gazette.*

PARLOA'S KITCHEN COMPANION.

A GUIDE FOR ALL WHO WOULD BE GOOD HOUSEKEEPERS.

Handsomely printed, and very fully illustrated. Large 8vo. (nearly 1000 pages). Neatly bound in extra cloth or in waterproof binding. - - - - - - - - $2.50

☞ It is thoroughly practical; it is perfectly reliable; it is marvellously comprehensive; it is copiously illustrated. It is, in short, overflowing with good qualities, and is just the book that all housekeepers need to guide them.

Miss Parloa's new book has proved a remarkable success, and it could hardly have been otherwise. Exhaustive in its treatment of a subject of the highest importance to all, the result of years of conscientious study and labor upon the part of one who has been called "the apostle of the *renaissance* in domestic service," it could not be otherwise than welcome to every intelligent housekeeper in the land.

"This is the most comprehensive volume that Miss Parloa has ever prepared, and, as a trusty companion and guide for all who are travelling on the road to good housekeeping, it must soon become a necessity. . . . . No amount of commendation seems to do justice to it."—*Good Housekeeper.*

PARLOA'S NEW COOK BOOK AND MARKETING GUIDE.

12mo. Cloth. - - - - - - - - - - $1.50

This is one of the most popular Cook Books ever printed, containing 1724 receipts and items of instruction. The directions are clear and concise, and the chapters on marketing and kitchen furnishing very useful.

ESTES & LAURIAT, PUBLISHERS,
BOSTON, MASS.

www.ingramcontent.com/pod-product-compliance
Lightning Source LLC
Chambersburg PA
CBHW030743230426
43667CB00007B/825